WOMAN'S DAY

GELATIN COOKERY

by Carole Collier

SIMON AND SCHUSTER
NEW YORK

Copyright © 1979 by CBS Consumer Publishing
All rights reserved
including the right of reproduction
in whole or in part in any form
Published by Simon and Schuster
A Division of Gulf & Western Corporation
Simon & Schuster Building
Rockefeller Center
1230 Avenue of the Americas
New York, New York 10020

Designed by Irving Perkins
Manufactured in the United States of America
1   2   3   4   5   6   7   8   9   10

Library of Congress Cataloging in Publication Data
Collier, Carole.
   Woman's day gelatin cookery.

   Includes index.
   1.   Cookery (Gelatin)   I.   Woman's day.
II.   Title.   III.   Title: Gelatin cookery.
TX814.5.G4C64   641.8′64   78–27638
ISBN 0–671–24749–2

To:

My dear friends Arnold I. Miller and Rae Gummel, of Children's Rights, Inc., 3443 17th Street, N.W., Washington, D.C. 20010, in thanks for their help to the victims of child-snatching, and for their efforts to protect children from this experience in the future;

And especially, to my daughter, Chantal, for her patience and interest in this book;

And to my son, Shane.

CONTENTS

FOREWORD, 9
CHOOSING THE CORRECT MOLD AND
   PREPARING IT FOR USE, 11
TIPS FOR SUCCESSFUL MOLDED GELATINS, 14
EASY UNMOLDING, 18
APPETIZERS, 21
MAIN COURSES—MEATS AND SEAFOOD, 48
VEGETABLE MOLDS, 88
FRUIT SALADS, 110
DECORATING MOLDED SALADS AND SAVORIES, 125
DECORATING DESSERTS, 144
RELISHES AND ACCOMPANIMENTS, 147
DESSERTS, 155
INTOXICATING DESSERTS, 201
CALORIE CONTROL AND DIET CONSCIOUSNESS, 219
NATURAL FOODS AND VEGETARIAN DIETS, 230

7

DO YOUR OWN THING, 235
TABLE OF MEASUREMENTS, 243
METRIC CONVERSIONS, 244
INDEX, 245

FOREWORD

Impressive molded gelatins are often thought of as being very difficult and time-consuming to prepare. I myself once believed that only very brave and experienced cooks could make them. A few years ago, however, I was asked to make the dessert for an "everybody contribute" dinner party. Wanting to outdo all the other contributors, I decided to make my very first charlotte.* I felt that since it would be surrounded by ladyfingers and the bottom of the mold would be lined with waxed paper, I could not fail when it came time for the great unmolding. Anxious and fearful, I held my breath, wondering if my efforts would collapse into a pile of mush. Lo and behold, it came out beautifully! I, of course, acted as though it was the easiest thing in the world to make,

* See page 12.

while I proudly accepted everyone's compliments. Reflecting in bed later that evening, I realized with wonder that indeed it *was* very easy—not only to make but to unmold. In fact, I marveled at the sturdiness of the dessert which looked so fragile. I became intrigued and began my venture into the world of molded gelatin cookery.

I was amazed at the advantages I discovered, spectacular, appetizing appearance being the most obvious. A turned-out gelatin is truly gratifying and impressive. Secondly, gelatins are do-ahead dishes. They can even be unmolded ahead of time and keep beautifully in the refrigerator for at least two or three days. Unlike other chilled dishes, gelatins need not be served directly from the refrigerator. A turned-out gelatin can be placed on the table at least an hour, sometimes longer, before serving time. In fact, the consistency of a creamy gelatin is often better if the mold is served at room temperature. Molded gelatins definitely meet the requirements for a buffet table. Lastly, although a moderate amount of time is necessary for their preparation, there is very little cooking involved—a boon in hot weather.

Many people have beautiful molds hanging as decorations on their kitchen walls and have never dared to use them. I sincerely believe that anyone, novice and gourmet cook alike, following the easy directions in this book will be delighted with the results.

CHOOSING THE CORRECT MOLD AND PREPARING IT FOR USE

First, choose the correct size mold for the quantity given in the recipe. You can determine the size of your mold by filling it with cups of water. You may use a mold if it varies neither more nor less than one cup from the quantity specified in the recipe; however, the exact size is preferred. (Note: Some recipes may be cut in half, but never attempt to double a recipe. It is better to make it twice in two molds.)

The shape of your mold can also be important. Deep, peaked or pointed cone molds are not suitable for gelatins made with a lot of cream, as they are difficult to turn out without spoiling the shape.

Surprisingly, there are probably many containers in your home which can make very attractive molds. Try cups, glasses, jars, bowls, vases, cans, dishes, or pans. Just make sure that the top and sides of the container are not smaller in circumference than the bottom, since that will make it impossible to turn out the gelatin.

To prepare a mold for use, first wash and dry it thoroughly. Pour into it a tablespoon or two of vegetable or salad oil. Rub the oil all around the inside of the mold with a piece of paper toweling, making sure not to miss any grooves and creases in the design. Molds should be *lightly* oiled; the paper toweling should absorb any excess oil as well as distribute it evenly. All molds that will contain a filling made with cream or mayonnaise should be oiled before use. (Note: Mayonnaise may be used as a substitute for the oil for gelatins made with mayonnaise.)

Molds that will hold a filling of clear jelly should not be oiled, but rather dipped in cold water. If oiled, the gelatin will come out with a clouded appearance. Each of the recipes in this book indicates which method to use in preparing your mold, oil or cold water.

A "charlotte" is *any* creamy gelatin dessert that has been formed in a charlotte mold lined with ladyfingers. Special charlotte molds available in gourmet shops are bucket-shaped, but a straight-sided soufflé dish will also serve the purpose. The straight sides are necessary to facilitate lining the mold with ladyfingers.

To prepare a charlotte mold for use: Line the bottom of the mold with waxed paper. Lightly oil the exposed surface of the paper (the side that will come in contact with the gelatin mixture). Do *not* oil the sides of the mold. Arrange the ladyfingers so that they are standing up and touching all around the inside of the mold. The ladyfingers should be placed rounded side out. The gelatin filling is then poured into the center.

A "soufflé" is *any* creamy gelatin (sweet or savory) that has been formed in a soufflé dish. This straight-sided dish is always several cups smaller than the quantity of gelatin placed inside it. Therefore, a "collar" of waxed paper must be tied or taped around the dish so that the paper extends 4 or 5 inches above the rim of the dish. This paper extension gives the extra height needed to hold the larger amount of gelatin placed inside the mold. Before serving, the paper collar is removed and the chilled gelatin will stand molded inside the dish.

Note: Do not use aluminum foil when making a paper collar. It creases too easily and will leave marks around the sides of the soufflé.

TIPS FOR SUCCESSFUL
MOLDED GELATINS

Softening Gelatin—Unflavored gelatin must first be softened in cold liquid for about 5 minutes before attempting to dissolve it with heat. If not softened, the granules tend to stick to the sides and bottom of the pan, and when placed over heat, they can easily become scorched. To soften, simply sprinkle the gelatin over or mix with the cold liquid called for in the recipe. The gelatin will absorb the liquid very quickly. If only a small amount of liquid is used for softening, it may all be absorbed, so do not become alarmed. This is quite normal.

It bears mentioning that there are one-step methods of dissolving gelatin that omit this presoftening time. One such way, which can only be used in preparing desserts, is to mix the gelatin in a saucepan with any sugar and salt called for in a recipe. The liquid is then added and heated immediately.

Because the gelatin granules are coated with the sugar and salt, they are less likely to stick to the bottom of the pan. In this manner, the softening time is omitted and you are saved the washing of an extra cup. However, the mixture must be stirred and attended from the moment the heat is applied. Another one-step method is to blend the gelatin with boiling liquid at high speed in a blender. This method has been demonstrated in "Doyle's Salmon Mousse" on page 84.

Flavored gelatin does not require pre-softening.

Dissolving Gelatin—There are several ways to dissolve gelatin, once it is softened, and details are given in each recipe. Whichever method is used, make sure the gelatin is completely dissolved (all granules melted), otherwise the mold may not get firm enough.

Chill Until Slightly Thickened—Before adding any solids, whipped cream or beaten egg whites, your gelatin mixture must be chilled until slightly thickened to insure an even distribution of the added ingredients. Otherwise, they might rise to the top or sink to the bottom. The correct consistency of a slightly thickened gelatin can be discerned by removing a large spoonful of the gelatin and letting it drop back into the bowl. If it forms a soft mound or is the consistency of unbeaten egg white, it is ready for the additions. When chilling until slightly thickened, always stir the gelatin mixture occasionally so that it will not lump together. If, by accident, the gelatin becomes very thick or set, place the bowl in a larger container of warm water and beat the gelatin until it returns to a smooth syrupy texture.

Layering Two or More Mixtures in the Same Mold—There are three important points to remember:

1. As each layer is poured into the mold, the gelatin must

be chilled until very thick before adding the next layer. This will prevent the mixtures from running together.

2. Although each chilled layer must set until very thick before adding the next layer, do not let it set completely. If an underlying layer is set too firmly, its overlying layer might slip off once the gelatin is unmolded. If, by accident, a chilled layer does become too firm, remove the mold from the refrigerator and allow the gelatin to reach room temperature before adding the next layer.

3. Make sure that the gelatin for each layer is completely cool before pouring it onto the layers that are already set. If the additional mixture is too warm, it may melt the layer beneath it and the two will run together.

Decorating from Within the Mold—When arranging a pattern or design in the bottom of a mold, it is necessary to do it in layered stages. Therefore, it is important to apply the three points of layering as mentioned above. The quantities of gelatin used in decorating are much smaller than those mentioned in the layering section, however. Therefore it is necessary to keep a very close watch over the chilling process. To facilitate this watch and to speed up the setting, simply place the mold in a large bowl half filled with ice and a little cold water. As the gelatin is added to the mold, it will set very quickly and enable you to lay out your design almost immediately, without chilling in the refrigerator.

Chill Until Firm—This will depend upon the size of the mold. Generally, one hour per each cup (4-cup mold, 4 hours) is sufficient. However, the longer a mold is chilled, the firmer it will be. Therefore, if time allows, let it chill for an extra hour or two beyond the minimum or even overnight.

Covering—Always cover any creamy gelatin with plastic wrap before chilling so that the other odors in the refrigerator are not absorbed by the gelatin. Clear gelatins should also be covered to prevent them from drying out and shrinking.

Freezing—Never attempt to freeze any leftover gelatin as freezing will make it turn very rubbery, or, in some cases, when frozen, it will crystallize and upon defrosting will melt into liquid. Leftover gelatin will keep nicely for several days if simply covered and placed in the refrigerator.

Grating—Some recipes call for the grating of vegetables or fruits. This is done to insure a good distribution of the ingredients and to facilitate slicing and serving. Gelatins that contain a quantity of grated foods, however, should be consumed within a day or two at most because gratings tend to bleed, or leak, their own juices, leaving an unsightly fluid on the serving dish.

Whipping or Beating—The purpose of whipping cream or egg whites is to add a fluffy and airy texture to the gelatin. Both cream and egg whites should be whipped until they are stiff enough to hold their shape or gently stand in peaks. Never beat to the point where cream or egg whites become dry, for then the gelatin will have a stodgy texture. Always whip or beat cream and egg whites just before adding them to the gelatin mixture. If they are prepared in advance, some of the air that has been beaten into them may be lost. A final point to remember: cream whips up easiest when it is chilled; egg whites whip up easiest when they are at room temperature.

Folding In—When a recipe calls for both whipped cream and beaten egg whites, the whipped cream, because it is the heavier of the two, should always be folded in first; the egg whites last.

EASY UNMOLDING

Method 1 (Warm Water)—Dip the mold up to about a half inch from the rim in warm (not hot) water for about 5 seconds. Carefully run a knife around the edge of the mold and give it a gentle *sideways* shake or two to loosen the gelatin. Place your serving dish on top of the mold and, holding both firmly together, turn them over (right side up). Shake the mold over or together with the serving dish from side to side (not up and down) until the gelatin slips out. If the gelatin doesn't come loose easily, try the warm dip again.

Method 2 (Warm Towel)—Carefully run a knife around the edge of the mold to loosen the gelatin. Place your serving dish on top of the mold and, holding both firmly together, turn them over (right side up). Soak a dish towel in warm (not hot) water and wring out. Place the warm cloth over and around the mold and hold it there for about 5 seconds. Remove the cloth and shake the mold gently over or together with the serving dish from side to side until the gelatin slips out. If the gelatin doesn't come loose easily, repeat the process.

Method 3 (Breaking the Air Lock)—Run a knife around the edge of the mold to loosen the gelatin. *Tilt* the mold in one hand and with the other insert the knife (at one point along the edge) down to the bottom of the mold while gently pulling the gelatin away from the side of the mold. This will break the air lock. Remove the knife. Place your serving dish over the top of the mold and, holding both firmly together, turn them over (right side up). Gently give the mold a sideways shake or two and the gelatin should slip out easily. If not, try breaking the air lock again. It is not necessary to do this all around the mold as releasing the vacuum at one spot should suffice. (Note: Never dip a creamy gelatin in warm water or use a warm towel to unmold it. This spoils the appearance by giving it a melted look. Always use Method 3 for creamy gelatins.)

Method 4 (Individual Molds)—Dip the mold up to the rim in warm (not hot) water. If possible, loosen the edges of the gelatin with the tip of a knife. Turn the mold over in your hand so that the filling can fall into your palm. Holding the mold in this position with one hand, use the knuckles of your other hand or the handle end of a small knife to sharply tap the bottom and sides of the mold until the gelatin drops out into your palm. If the gelatin does not drop out easily, try the warm-water dip and tapping process again.

Method 5 (Metal Can)—Empty metal cans can be used to mold gelatins. If you have made a creamy gelatin, puncture the bottom of the can, loosen the sides of the gelatin, and invert the can onto the serving dish. If you have made a clear gelatin, loosen the sides of the gelatin, dip the can in warm water, then puncture the bottom of the can and invert it onto the serving dish. It is the puncturing of the can that releases the air lock and makes the gelatin slip out on its own power. Give a sideways shake or two if necessary.

Method 6 (Charlotte Molds)—Run a knife or spatula around the sides of the mold to loosen the gelatin. (Some gelatin may have seeped through the ladyfingers.) Place the serving dish over the top of the mold and, holding both firmly together, turn them over (right side up). Since the bottom of the mold was lined with waxed paper, the charlotte should immediately come free of the mold. Carefully remove the waxed paper before serving.

Method 7 (Soufflés)—Soufflés are not unmolded. They are meant to be served in the dish in which they were formed. Simply untie and remove the paper collar before serving.

APPETIZERS

In general, most cooks prepare appetizers and hors d'oeuvres only when entertaining. At such a time, molded gelatins are ideal not only because they can be prepared ahead of time but also because they are very impressive-looking. Instead of the ordinary dip, it is just as easy and much more attractive to prepare a molded mousse spread. Serve molded gelatins with chips, crackers, toast, or fresh vegetable dippers: celery, carrots, green pepper, cauliflowerets, cucumber sticks, zucchini sticks.

The simplest foods can be presented as a most elegant first course, especially when turned out in individual molds.

This chapter contains recipes that not only can be used as appetizers and first courses, but many are suitable for pleasing light luncheon dishes.

ANCHOVY-ARTICHOKE ASPIC
(6-cup mold, dipped in cold water)

3½ cups tomato juice
2 bay leaves
2 cloves
1 onion, diced
¼ teaspoon salt
Dash pepper
2 packages (3 ounces each) lemon-flavored gelatin
1 jar (6 ounces) marinated artichoke hearts, drained and
   chopped
1 jar (4 ounces) sliced pimientos, drained and chopped
2 cans (2 ounces each) flat fillets of anchovies, drained and
   minced

In a medium saucepan, combine the tomato juice, bay leaves, cloves, onion, salt, and pepper. Bring to a boil and simmer for 15 minutes. Strain and pour over the gelatin. Stir until gelatin is dissolved. Chill until slightly thickened, stirring occasionally.

Combine the chopped artichokes, pimientos, and anchovies. Stir into the thickened aspic, mixing well. Turn into the prepared mold and chill until set.

Unmold, using Method 1 or 2.

Serve as a molded spread accompanied with crackers.

CAVIAR MOUSSE
(5-cup mold, lightly oiled)

1 envelope unflavored gelatin
Juice of 1 lemon plus water to make ¼ cup liquid
7-ounce jar red lumpfish caviar
¼ cup finely chopped parsley

1 tablespoon grated onion
Grated rind of 1 lemon
2 cups sour cream
⅛ teaspoon cayenne pepper
1 cup heavy cream, whipped

Sprinkle gelatin over liquid in a heat-resistant cup and let stand for 5 minutes to soften. Place cup in a pan of hot water over low heat, stirring until gelatin is dissolved. Cool slightly.

Combine caviar, parsley, onion, lemon rind, sour cream, and cayenne pepper. Add cooled gelatin to caviar mixture and blend well. Fold in whipped cream. Turn into prepared mold and chill until set.

Unmold, using Method 3.

MOLDED CELERY RÉMOULADES
(6–8 individual molds, lightly oiled)

1 envelope unflavored gelatin
¼ cup cold water
1 tablespoon prepared mustard
1 tablespoon lemon juice
1¼ cups mayonnaise
1 cup sour cream
4 medium celery knobs, peeled and grated
Salt and pepper to taste

In a small heat-resistant cup, sprinkle the gelatin over the cold water and let stand 5 minutes to soften. Place cup in a pan of hot water over low heat, stirring until gelatin is dissolved.

Combine the mustard, lemon juice, mayonnaise, and sour cream in a mixing bowl. Add the dissolved gelatin and whisk until well blended. Chill until slightly thickened, stirring occasionally.

Prepare the celery while the gelatin mixture is chilling. Add it to the thickened mixture with salt and pepper to taste. Turn into the prepared molds and chill until set.

Unmold, using Method 3 or 4.

Serve on individual beds of lettuce.

THREE CHEESE RING

(3½-cup ring mold, lightly oiled)

1 pound creamed cottage cheese
2 packages (3 ounces each) cream cheese, softened
4 ounces blue cheese, mashed
1 envelope unflavored gelatin
¼ cup cold water
1 small onion, grated
1 teaspoon Worcestershire sauce
1 tablespoon lemon juice
Salt and cayenne pepper to taste
Crisp vegetable dippers, chilled (for garnish)

Combine the three cheeses and blend well.

Sprinkle the gelatin over the water in a heat-resistant cup and let stand for 5 minutes to soften. Place cup in a pan of hot water over low heat, stirring until gelatin is dissolved. Add to the mixed cheeses. Blend in the onion, Worcestershire sauce, lemon juice, salt, and pepper and taste for seasoning. Turn into the prepared mold and chill until set.

Unmold, using Method 1 or 2. Garnish with chilled crisp vegetable dippers.

Serve with additional chilled crisp vegetable dippers.

CHICKEN DIABLO MOUSSE
(6-cup mold, lightly oiled)

1 envelope unflavored gelatin
1/4 cup dry white wine
1 cup chicken broth
1 tablespoon grated onion
2 tablespoons grated celery
2 tablespoons Dijon mustard
4 drops hot pepper sauce
1/2 cup sour cream
Salt and pepper to taste
2 cups ground cooked chicken
1 cup heavy cream, whipped

Sprinkle the gelatin over the wine in a heat-resistant cup and let stand for 5 minutes to soften. Place cup in a pan of hot water over low heat, stirring until gelatin is dissolved. Add to the chicken broth. Add the onion, celery, mustard, pepper sauce, sour cream, and salt and pepper to taste. Mix well. Chill until slightly thickened, stirring occasionally.

Add the chicken and fold in the whipped cream. Turn into the prepared mold and chill until set.

Unmold, using Method 3.

BRANDIED CHICKEN LIVER PÂTÉ
(4-cup mold, lightly oiled)

    1 envelope unflavored gelatin
    ¼ cup cold water
    1 pound fresh chicken livers
    Flour
    3 tablespoons bacon fat
    ½ pound fresh mushrooms, sliced
    1 tablespoon chopped onion
    2 cloves garlic, minced
    1 cup chicken broth
    1 teaspoon dry mustard
    ½ teaspoon salt
    ¼ teaspoon nutmeg
    ⅛ teaspoon pepper
    ⅛ teaspoon ground cloves
    ¼ cup brandy
    ¼ cup mayonnaise
    ½ cup heavy cream, whipped

Soften the gelatin in the cold water. Dredge the chicken livers lightly in flour. Melt the bacon fat in a frying pan. Add the chicken livers and sauté gently until browned on all sides. Add the mushrooms, onion, and garlic and sauté until soft. Add the chicken broth; cover and simmer gently until the livers are cooked through. Remove from heat and strain. Stir the gelatin in the hot broth until gelatin is dissolved.

Cut the livers into quarters. Add the spices and brandy to the liver-mushroom mixture. Make a purée in a blender, using the liver-mushroom mixture, the mayonnaise, and all the gelatin broth. Turn into a mixing bowl and chill until slightly thickened, stirring occasionally.

Fold in the whipped cream. Turn into the prepared mold and chill until set.

Unmold, using Method 3.

Serve with toast triangles.

CLAM DIP MOUSSE
($4\frac{1}{2}$-cup mold, lightly oiled)

1 envelope unflavored gelatin
Liquid drained from clams
$\frac{1}{4}$ cup dry white wine
1 envelope ($1\frac{1}{2}$ ounces) dry onion soup mix
1 cup sour cream
1 can ($10\frac{1}{2}$ ounces) minced clams, drained
1 cup heavy cream, whipped

Sprinkle the gelatin over the clam liquid and white wine in a heat-resistant cup and let stand for 5 minutes to soften. Place cup in a pan of hot water over low heat, stirring until gelatin is dissolved. Combine the onion soup mix with the sour cream and add the dissolved gelatin. Chill until slightly thickened.

Add the clams and fold in the whipped cream. Turn into the prepared mold and chill until set.

Unmold, using Method 3.

CLAM RING
(5-cup ring mold, lightly oiled)

1 envelope unflavored gelatin
½ cup clam juice
1 cup tomato juice
8 ounces cream cheese, diced
½ cup mayonnaise
1 tablespoon lemon juice
½ cup finely chopped celery
¼ cup finely chopped onion
¼ cup finely chopped green pepper
1½ cups cooked minced clams
Salt and pepper to taste

Soften the gelatin in the clam juice. Heat the tomato juice and add the cream cheese gradually, stirring until smooth. Add the gelatin, stirring until gelatin is dissolved. Remove from heat and add the mayonnaise and lemon juice. Chill until slightly thickened, stirring occasionally.

Add the remaining ingredients to the thickened gelatin and taste for seasoning. Turn into the prepared mold and chill until set.

Unmold, using Method 3.

COTTAGE CLAM MOUSSE
(5-cup mold, lightly oiled)

1 envelope plus 1 teaspoon unflavored gelatin
½ cup clam juice
1 egg, separated
½ cup milk
¼ teaspoon salt
⅛ teaspoon white pepper
1 tablespoon lemon juice
1 teaspoon grated lemon rind
1 tablespoon grated onion
1½ cups creamed cottage cheese
1 can (10½ ounces) minced clams, drained
½ cup heavy cream, whipped

Soften the gelatin in the clam juice. In the top of a double boiler, beat the egg yolk with the milk. Stir in the softened gelatin. Cook over hot water, stirring constantly until slightly thickened. Cool.

Add the salt, pepper, lemon juice, rind, onion, and cottage cheese. Chill until cold and slightly thickened, stirring occasionally.

Beat the egg white until stiff. Fold the clams and whipped cream into the thickened mixture. Fold in the egg white. Turn into the prepared mold and chill until set.

Unmold, using Method 3.

EGG MOUSSE
(6-cup mold, lightly oiled)

1 envelope plus 1½ teaspoons unflavored gelatin
1 cup cold chicken broth
1 cup milk
1 slice onion
1 bay leaf
4 peppercorns
1 tablespoon butter
1 tablespoon flour
¼ teaspoon Worcestershire sauce
¼ teaspoon anchovy paste
6 hard-cooked eggs, separated
1 cup sour cream
Salt and cayenne pepper to taste
½ cup heavy cream, whipped
Black caviar (for garnish)
Toast triangles (for garnish)

Soften the gelatin in the cold chicken broth. Scald the milk with the onion, bay leaf, and peppercorns. Melt the butter in a saucepan. Add the flour, stirring to form a smooth paste. Remove from heat. Strain the hot milk and add it to the flour paste, stirring until smooth. Place over low heat until the mixture thickens slightly, stirring constantly. Stir in the softened gelatin and continue cooking over low heat until gelatin is dissolved. Remove from heat. Add the Worcester-shire and anchovy paste. Chill until slightly thickened, stirring occasionally.

Force the egg yolks through a sieve and beat them with the sour cream. Add the thickened gelatin and continue beating until smooth. Add the salt and cayenne; taste for seasoning. Finely mince the egg whites and add to the mixture. Fold in the whipped cream. Turn into the prepared mold and chill until set.

Unmold, using Method 3. Garnish with the black caviar and toast triangles.

Serve with additional black caviar and toast triangles.

CURRIED EGG CUPS
(6 individual molds, lightly oiled)

1 envelope plus 1 teaspoon unflavored gelatin
1 can (10½ ounces) chicken broth
1 tablespoon curry powder
1 tablespoon finely minced chutney
1 tablespoon grated onion
1 teaspoon salt
1 cup mayonnaise
½ cup sour cream
6 hard-cooked eggs, peeled and cooled
Pimientos (for garnish)

Sprinkle gelatin over the chicken broth in a saucepan and let stand for 5 minutes to soften. Stir constantly over low heat until the gelatin is dissolved. Turn off heat and set gelatin mixture aside to cool.

In a bowl, combine curry powder, chutney, onion, salt, mayonnaise, and sour cream. Add gelatin mixture and taste for seasoning. Pour just enough of this sauce into each mold to cover the bottom. Chill until set.

Place an egg in each mold and spoon the remaining sauce over them. Garnish each with a pimiento strip and chill until set.

Unmold, using Method 3 or 4.

EGGS WITH ASPARAGUS MOUSSE
(4 individual molds, lightly oiled)

   1 envelope unflavored gelatin
   Asparagus liquid plus enough water to make 1 cup
   1 can (14½ ounces) asparagus spears, drained and sieved
      through a food mill
   ½ cup mayonnaise
   1 teaspoon Worcestershire sauce
   1 teaspoon lemon juice
   1 cup heavy cream, whipped
   4 eggs, firmly poached (or boiled, cooled, and peeled)
   1 small can asparagus tips (for garnish)

Sprinkle the gelatin over the liquid (1 cup) in a small saucepan and let stand for 5 minutes to soften. Stir over low heat until gelatin is dissolved.

Combine the sieved asparagus with the mayonnaise, Worcestershire sauce, and lemon juice. Add the gelatin and taste for seasoning. Chill until slightly thickened, stirring occasionally.

Fold in the whipped cream. Pour a thin layer of mousse into the bottom of each mold and chill until set.

Place an egg in each mold and cover with the remaining mousse. Chill until set.

Unmold, using Method 3 or 4. Garnish with asparagus tips.

INDIVIDUAL EGGS IN AVOCADO MOUSSE
(4 individual molds, lightly oiled)

   1 envelope unflavored gelatin
   1 cup chicken broth, divided
   1 large avocado

1 teaspoon lemon juice
Salt to taste
Chili powder to taste
1 cup sour cream
4 eggs, firmly poached (or boiled, cooled, and peeled)

Sprinkle gelatin over ½ cup of chicken broth in a saucepan and let stand for 5 minutes to soften. Stir constantly over low heat until the gelatin is dissolved. Turn off heat and set mixture aside to cool.

In a blender, purée the avocado with the remaining ½ cup chicken broth. Add the purée, lemon juice, salt, and chili powder to the sour cream and mix well. Add the gelatin mixture. Pour just enough of this sauce into each mold to cover the bottom. Chill until set.

Place an egg in each mold and spoon the remaining sauce over them. Chill until set.

Unmold, using Method 3 or 4.

EGG SALAD MOLD
(3-cup mold, lightly oiled)

1 envelope unflavored gelatin
¼ cup cold water
1 cup milk
1 teaspoon salt
1 teaspoon prepared mustard
1 tablespoon ketchup
½ cup mayonnaise
½ cup sour cream
6 hard-cooked eggs, finely chopped
Salad greens (for garnish)

In a small heat-resistant cup, sprinkle the gelatin over the cold water and let stand for 5 minutes to soften. Place cup in a pan of hot water over low heat, constantly stirring until gelatin is dissolved.

In a mixing bowl, add the dissolved gelatin to the milk. Add the salt, stirring until salt is dissolved. Add the mustard, ketchup, mayonnaise, and sour cream. Whisk until blended. Taste for seasoning. Chill until slightly thickened, stirring occasionally.

Stir in the chopped eggs. Turn into the prepared mold and chill until set.

Unmold, using Method 3. Garnish with greens.

Serve with crackers.

Variation

CURRIED EGG SALAD MOLD

Add curry powder to taste when combining all the ingredients.

GUACAMOUSSE
(5-cup mold, lightly oiled)

> 1 package (3 ounces) lime-flavored gelatin
> 1 cup boiling water
> 2 large ripe avocados, sieved or mashed
> 1 tablespoon grated onion
> 1 clove garlic, crushed
> 2 tablespoons lemon juice
> 1½ teaspoons salt
> ½ teaspoon chili powder
> 2 green chili peppers, finely chopped
> 1 tomato, skinned and chopped
> 1 cup heavy cream, whipped

Dissolve the gelatin in the boiling water. Cool slightly.

Combine the avocado purée, onion, garlic, lemon juice, salt, and chili powder and mix well. Add the gelatin and beat until well blended. Chill until slightly thickened, stirring occasionally.

Add the chili peppers and tomato. Fold in the whipped cream. Turn into the prepared mold and chill until set.

Unmold, using Method 3.

Serve with corn chips.

FRESH HERB MOUSSE
(2½-cup mold, lightly oiled)

2 teaspoons unflavored gelatin
¼ cup cold water
1 tablespoon lemon juice
⅛ teaspoon salt
2 tablespoons prepared Dijon mustard
2 teaspoons paprika
1 clove garlic, crushed
½ cup fresh snipped dill
¼ cup fresh snipped parsley
1 cup sour cream
½ cup heavy cream, whipped

In a heat-resistant cup, sprinkle the gelatin over the cold water and let stand for 5 minutes to soften. Place cup in a pan of hot water over low heat, stirring until gelatin is dissolved. Add the lemon juice and salt and stir until salt is dissolved. Set aside to cool.

In a mixing bowl, combine the mustard, paprika, garlic, dill, and parsley with the sour cream. Add the dissolved gelatin and whisk until smooth. Fold in the heavy cream. Turn into the prepared mold and chill until set.

Unmold, using Method 3.

This mousse should be served as a spread accompanied with crackers or fresh vegetable dippers.

HORSERADISH–CREAM CHEESE MOUSSE
(3-cup mold, lightly oiled)

1 envelope unflavored gelatin
¾ cup cold milk
2 packages (3 ounces each) cream cheese, softened
3 tablespoons fresh grated horseradish
¼ teaspoon paprika
3 drops hot pepper sauce
2 tablespoons finely chopped parsley
½ cup sour cream
Salt and pepper to taste
½ cup heavy cream, whipped

Sprinkle the gelatin on the milk in a saucepan and let stand for 5 minutes to soften. Heat, stirring until gelatin is dissolved (do not boil). Remove from heat. Dice the cream cheese and add to the hot milk. Beat with a rotary beater until smooth. Add the horseradish, paprika, pepper sauce, parsley, sour cream, salt, and pepper. Mix well. Chill until slightly thickened, stirring occasionally.

Fold in the whipped cream. Turn into the prepared mold and chill until set.

Unmold, using Method 3.

JAMBON PERSILLE (PARSLIED HAM)
(8-cup mold, dipped in cold water)

2 envelopes unflavored gelatin
¾ cup dry white wine
2¾ cups chicken or veal stock, fat removed
⅛ teaspoon nutmeg
¼ teaspoon thyme
½ teaspoon tarragon
1 bay leaf
2 tablespoons lemon juice or tarragon vinegar
Salt and pepper to taste
4 cups diced cooked ham
1 cup minced fresh parsley
Sprigs of parsley (for garnish)

In a medium-sized bowl, soften the gelatin in the white wine. In a medium-sized saucepan, combine the stock, nutmeg, thyme, tarragon, and bay leaf. Bring to a boil, lower heat and simmer gently for 10 minutes. Strain into the bowl containing the softened gelatin and stir until gelatin is dissolved. Taste for seasoning and add lemon juice or tarragon vinegar, salt and pepper, if desired. Chill, stirring occasionally, until the mixture is cold and slightly syrupy.

Combine the ham and minced parsley. Fold into the syrupy gelatin. Turn into the prepared mold and chill until set.

Unmold, using Method 1 or 2. Garnish with parsley sprigs. Serve with a cold mustard sauce.

LIVERWURST MOUSSE IN ASPIC
(6-cup mold, lightly oil the sides of the mold only)

1 envelope unflavored gelatin
2 cups beef consommé, divided
1 tablespoon brandy or sherry
Pistachio nuts, shelled and skinned (for decoration)
2 cups (1 pound) liverwurst*
8-ounce cream cheese, softened
1 tablespoon grated onion
1/4 cup chopped pistachio nuts
1/2 cup heavy cream, whipped

Make an aspic: Sprinkle the gelatin over 1/4 cup of consommé in a small heat-resistant cup and let stand 5 minutes to soften. Place cup in a pan of hot water over low heat, stirring until gelatin is dissolved. Add to the remaining consommé and the brandy. Chill until cold and syrupy in consistency.

Cover the bottom of the prepared mold with a thin layer of the aspic and chill until set.

When aspic is firm to touch, arrange a design with the pistachio nuts and carefully ladle another thin layer of the syrupy aspic into the mold to set the pattern. Chill.

Mash the liverwurst and combine with the cream cheese and onion. Beat in the remaining aspic. Add the chopped nuts and fold in the whipped cream. Turn into the patterned mold and chill until set.

Unmold, using Method 1 or 2.

* Goose liverwurst (Braunschweiger) is best, if available.

CREAMY ONION MOUSSE
(3-cup mold, lightly oiled)

1 envelope unflavored gelatin
¼ cup cold water
1 envelope (1½ ounces) dry onion soup mix
1 cup sour cream
1 cup heavy cream, whipped

Sprinkle the gelatin over the water in a heat-resistant cup and let stand for 5 minutes to soften. Place cup in a pan of hot water over low heat, stirring until gelatin is dissolved.

Combine the soup mix with the sour cream and add the gelatin. Fold in the whipped cream. Turn into the prepared mold and chill until set.

Unmold, using Method 3.

PÂTÉ MOUSSE
(4-cup mold, lightly oiled)

2 teaspoons unflavored gelatin
½ cup cold water
2 cups mashed pâté (foie gras)
¼ cup finely chopped raisins
2 tablespoons sherry or brandy
½ cup heavy cream, whipped

Sprinkle the gelatin over the water in a small heat-resistant cup and let stand for 5 minutes to soften. Place cup in a pan of hot water over low heat, stirring until gelatin is dissolved. Add to the pâté and beat until smooth. Chill slightly.

Soak the raisins in the sherry. Add to the gelatin pâté. Fold in the whipped cream. Turn into the prepared mold and chill until set.

Unmold, using Method 3.

MOLDED QUICHE LAFAYETTE
(8″ x 8″ pan, lightly oiled, or 8 individual molds, lightly oiled)

> 1 can (4 ounces) mushroom stems and pieces, drained (reserve liquid)
> 1 can (7 ounces) whole-kernel corn, drained (reserve liquid)
> 1 envelope unflavored gelatin
> 3 egg yolks
> 1 cup milk
> 2 triangles Gruyère cheese, grated
> 3 tablespoons grated Parmesan cheese
> 1 tablespoon grated onion
> ¼ teaspoon cayenne pepper
> ½ teaspoon salt
> ½ cup finely chopped boiled ham
> 1 cup heavy cream, whipped

Combine the mushroom and corn liquids. Sprinkle the gelatin over the combined liquids and let stand for 5 minutes to soften.

In a small saucepan, lightly beat the egg yolks with the milk. Place over low heat, stirring constantly until the mixture begins to thicken slightly (do not boil). Add the Gruyère and Parmesan, stirring until both are melted and smooth. Remove from heat. Stir in the softened gelatin until it is dissolved. Add the onion, pepper, and salt. Chill until slightly thickened, stirring occasionally.

Add the mushrooms, corn, and ham. Fold in the whipped

cream. Turn into the prepared pan or individual molds. Chill until set.

If using an 8" x 8" pan, unmold by Method 3. Cut into squares and serve on crackers.

If using individual molds, unmold by Method 4.

Variations

QUICHE LORRAINE

Use 8 ounces of mushroom stems and pieces and omit the corn. Increase quantity of ham to 1 cup.

SHRIMP OR CRABMEAT QUICHE

Omit the corn and ham, substituting 1½ cups chopped cooked shrimp or crab meat. Add 2 tablespoons sherry to the mushroom liquid, to replace the corn liquid which has been omitted.

SPANISH QUICHE

Omit the mushrooms and corn. Add ¼ cup cold milk to replace the mushroom and corn liquids. Add 1 ripe tomato (peeled, seeded, and chopped), ¾ cup chopped black olives, ½ green bell pepper (seeded, blanched, and chopped). A few drops of hot pepper sauce may be added for a spicy flavor, if desired.

RED AND WHITE RING
(5-cup ring mold, lightly oiled)

WHITE LAYER

1 envelope unflavored gelatin
½ cup cold milk
2 cups cottage cheese
¼ cup snipped chives
1 tablespoon chopped parsley
1 teaspoon salt
⅛ teaspoon cayenne pepper

RED LAYER

1 envelope unflavored gelatin
2 cups V-8 (or similar) juice, divided
1 tablespoon lemon juice

WHITE LAYER

Sprinkle the gelatin over the cold milk in a small heat-resistant cup and let stand for 5 minutes to soften. Place cup in a pan of hot water over low heat, stirring until gelatin is dissolved. Set aside to cool.

In a mixing bowl, combine the remaining ingredients for the white layer. Add the gelatin. Mix well. Turn into the prepared mold and chill. (See Tips on Layering, pages 15–16.)

RED LAYER

Sprinkle the gelatin over ¼ cup of the V-8 juice in a small heat-resistant cup and let stand for 5 minutes to soften. Place cup in a pan of hot (not boiling) water over low heat, stirring until gelatin is dissolved. Add to the remaining juice. Add the lemon juice and mix well. Chill until slightly thickened.

Turn into the mold, carefully pouring over the white layer. Chill until firm.

Unmold, using Method 1 or 2.

ROQUEFORT CHEESE MOUSSE
(3½-cup mold, lightly oiled)

  1 envelope unflavored gelatin
  1 cup cold milk
  4 ounces Roquefort cheese, mashed
  2 tablespoons lemon juice
  2 tablespoons chopped parsley
  1 teaspoon grated onion
  ¼ teaspoon salt
  ⅛ teaspoon cayenne pepper
  1 cup heavy cream, whipped

Sprinkle the gelatin on top of the milk in a saucepan and heat, stirring until gelatin is dissolved (do not boil). Add the cheese to the hot milk and beat with a rotary beater until blended. Add the lemon juice, parsley, onion, salt, and pepper. Chill until slightly thickened, stirring occasionally.

Fold in the whipped cream. Turn into the prepared mold and chill until set.

Unmold, using Method 3.

SALMON-CAVIAR MOUSSE
(5-cup mold, lightly oiled)

  1 envelope unflavored gelatin
  1 can (1 pound) red salmon, drained (reserve liquid)
  Juice of 1 lemon
  Grated rind of 1 lemon
  1 tablespoon grated onion
  4 drops hot pepper sauce
  3½ ounces red caviar
  1 cup sour cream
  ½ cup heavy cream, whipped

Sprinkle the gelatin over the salmon liquid in a heat-resistant cup and let stand for 5 minutes to soften. Place cup in a pan of hot water over low heat, stirring until gelatin is dissolved.

Force the salmon through a food mill or purée in a blender.* Combine the lemon juice, rind, onion, pepper sauce, caviar, and sour cream in a mixing bowl. Add the salmon purée. Stir in the dissolved gelatin. Chill until slightly thickened, stirring occasionally.

Fold in the whipped cream. Turn into the prepared mold and chill until set.

Unmold, using Method 3.

SALMON MOUSSE WITH SHRIMP
(2½-cup mold, lightly oiled)

    1 envelope unflavored gelatin
    ¼ cup cold water
    1 can (7¾ ounces) red salmon, drained (reserve liquid)
    ¼ cup mayonnaise
    1 tablespoon lemon juice
    1 tablespoon grated onion
    2½-ounce jar tiny shrimp, drained (reserve liquid)
    1 tablespoon brandy
    ½ cup heavy cream, whipped

Sprinkle the gelatin over the water in a heat-resistant cup and let stand for 5 minutes to soften. Place cup in a pan of hot water over low heat, stirring until gelatin is dissolved.

In a blender, purée the drained salmon with the mayonnaise, lemon juice, and grated onion. Turn puréed mixture into a mixing bowl. Add the reserved liquids and the dissolved gelatin. Chill until slightly thickened.

---

* If the salmon is puréed in a blender, the lemon juice and dissolved gelatin may be added at that time.

Sprinkle the brandy over the shrimp and let stand while the salmon mixture is chilling.

Add the shrimp and fold in the whipped cream. Turn into the prepared mold and chill until set.

Unmold, using Method 3.

SMOKED SALMON MOUSSE
(4 cup mold, lightly oiled)

1 envelope unflavored gelatin
Juice of 1 lemon plus water to make ¼ cup liquid
12 ounces smoked salmon, shredded
1 cup sour cream
½ teaspoon capers
¼ teaspoon cayenne pepper
1 cup heavy cream, whipped

Sprinkle gelatin over liquid in a heat-resistant cup and let stand for 5 minutes to soften. Place cup in a pan of hot water over low heat, stirring until gelatin is dissolved. Cool slightly.

In a blender, purée the salmon with the sour cream, capers, and cayenne pepper for 15 seconds. Add cooled gelatin to salmon purée. Blend for 10 seconds. Turn into a mixing bowl. Fold in the whipped cream. Turn into prepared mold and chill until set.

Unmold, using Method 3.

SHRIMP IN BRANDIED ASPIC
(4 individual molds, dipped in cold water)

  1 envelope unflavored gelatin
  2 cups seasoned fish stock, strained and divided
  1 tablespoon brandy or cognac
  2 stuffed green olives, cut in half
  ½ pound medium-sized shrimp, cooked and peeled

Sprinkle the gelatin over ½ cup of fish stock in a small heat-resistant dish and let stand for 5 minutes to soften. Place dish in a pan of hot water over low heat, stirring until gelatin is dissolved. Add this to the remaining 1½ cups stock. Stir in the brandy. Pour a thin layer of this aspic into each mold and chill until very thick. (See Tips on Decorating, page 16.)

Place an olive half (cut side down) in the center of each mold on top of the set gelatin. Arrange 2 shrimp around each olive. Carefully ladle another layer of aspic over the design to set the pattern. Chill until set.

Cut the remaining shrimp into thirds and divide equally among each of the 4 molds on top of the set pattern. Pour in the remaining aspic. Chill until set.

Unmold, using Method 4.

Serve each shrimp aspic on a leaf of lettuce, or surround with watercress.

SHRIMP-AND-TOMATO CREAM MOUSSE
(4-cup mold, lightly oiled)

  1 envelope unflavored gelatin
  1 cup tomato juice
  1 cup bottled clam juice
  1 tablespoon lemon juice
  1 carrot, peeled and grated on medium hole

1 medium onion, grated
1 cup cooked baby shrimp or 2 cans (4½ ounces each) small
    shrimp, drained
½ cup heavy cream, whipped

In a saucepan, sprinkle the gelatin over the tomato juice and
let stand for 5 minutes to soften. Place over medium heat and
stir until gelatin is dissolved. Remove from heat. Add clam
juice and lemon juice. Chill until slightly thickened, stirring
occasionally.

Stir in the carrot, onion, and shrimp until well mixed. Fold
in the whipped cream. Turn into the prepared mold and
chill until set.

Unmold, using Method 3.

INDIVIDUAL WINE-CONSOMMÉ MOLDS
(6 individual molds, lightly oiled)

2 envelopes unflavored gelatin
3 cups beef consommé
1 cup dry red wine
1 teaspoon sugar
1 teaspoon lemon juice
Salt and pepper
1 red onion, sliced (for garnish)
Watercress (for garnish)

Sprinkle the gelatin over the consommé in a saucepan and
stir over low heat until gelatin is dissolved. Cool slightly.

Add the wine, sugar, lemon juice, salt, and pepper. Turn
into 6 prepared individual molds. Chill until set.

Unmold, using Method 4. Top each mold with a thin slice
of red onion garnished with watercress.

MAIN COURSES—
MEATS AND SEAFOOD

Most cooks today don't seem to find enough minutes in the day to devote the time they'd like to preparing attractive foods. At first thought, with lengthy preparation in mind, one might tend to shy away from molded main courses. However, there are many valid reasons why these should be included quite regularly in the weekly meal planning, especially during hot weather.

All these recipes can be prepared ahead of time, the night before, if desired, when it is cooler and you are less rushed. The preparation time involved is actually relatively short, in most cases, and it is only the final chilling process that is time-consuming, but that step does not require any attention.

Economy, too, should be considered. Molded main courses are a great way to use leftovers, and when mixed with other ingredients, even small amounts can provide another whole meal.

JELLIED BEEF À LA MODE
(5- to 6-cup mold, dipped in cold water)

2 pounds of beef for stew
1 tablespoon oil or bacon fat
Salt and pepper
1 cup water
2 cups dry white wine
1 tablespoon soy sauce
1 whole clove garlic, peeled
2 whole small onions, peeled
1 carrot, washed and cut in 2-inch pieces
2 tablespoons chopped parsley
2 tablespoons brandy
1 envelope unflavored gelatin
Sprigs of parsley (for garnish)

Cut beef in 1-inch cubes, discarding any fat. Heat oil in a heavy pot until hot. On high heat, *quickly* brown meat on all sides. Season meat with salt and pepper. Add water, wine, and soy sauce. Bring to a boil. Turn to low heat; add garlic, onions, and carrot pieces. Cover and simmer until meat is tender, about 1½ to 2 hours.

Strain the cooking liquid into a large measuring cup. Remove garlic, onions, and carrots from the meat and discard them. Sprinkle the meat with the chopped parsley and brandy; cover and refrigerate. Refrigerate the liquid until cold and the fat coagulates at the top. (This may also be done in the freezer.)

Remove the fat; take note of how much liquid remains.

Place liquid in a small saucepan. Sprinkle the gelatin over the cold liquid and let stand for 5 minutes to soften. Heat liquid over medium heat, stirring until gelatin is dissolved. Two cups of liquid are needed. If you do not have enough, add water. If you have an excess, boil the liquid down to 2 cups. Chill until slightly thickened, stirring occasionally.

Fold the chilled meat mixture into the slightly thickened gelatin. Turn into the prepared mold and chill until set.

Unmold, using Method 1 or 2. Garnish with parsley sprigs.

CITRUS RING WITH CHICKEN-ALMOND SALAD
(4-cup ring mold, dipped in cold water)

2 envelopes unflavored gelatin
1½ cups tomato juice, divided
2 cups orange juice
¼ cup lemon juice
¼ teaspoon salt
½ teaspoon Worcestershire sauce
Chicken-Almond Salad (recipe follows)

In a small heat-resistant cup, sprinkle gelatin over ½ cup of tomato juice and let stand 5 minutes to soften. Place in a pan of hot water, over low heat, gently stirring until dissolved. Combine the remaining tomato juice, the orange juice, lemon juice, salt and Worcestershire and add the dissolved gelatin. Turn into the prepared mold and chill until set.

Unmold, using Method 1 or 2. Fill ring with Chicken-Almond Salad and garnish with fresh salad greens.

Note: The Citrus Ring recipe may be doubled by increasing the amount of gelatin to 4 envelopes plus 1½ teaspoons. In that case, use an 8-cup ring mold.

CHICKEN-ALMOND SALAD

In a large bowl, mix 4 cups cubed cooked chicken and 2 cups sliced celery. Blend ¾ cup mayonnaise, ½ cup sour cream, 1 tablespoon lemon juice, ½ teaspoon salt and dash of pepper; add to chicken mixture and toss lightly. Gently fold in ½ cup toasted slivered almonds and 1 cup halved seedless green grapes. Chill thoroughly.

CURRIED APPLE-CHICKEN MOUSSE
(8-cup mold, lightly oiled)

    2 envelopes unflavored gelatin
    ½ cup white wine
    2 cups chicken broth
    3 tablespoons lemon juice
    1 teaspoon dry mustard
    2 teaspoons curry powder*
    1 teaspoon salt
    1 tablespoon grated onion
    ½ teaspoon sugar
    2 cups sour cream
    2 cups finely chopped cooked chicken
    ½ cup finely chopped celery
    2 Delicious (red) apples, washed

Sprinkle gelatin over the wine and let stand for 5 minutes to soften. Bring broth to a boil. Turn off heat and add gelatin, stirring until gelatin is dissolved. Set aside to cool.

In a mixing bowl, combine lemon juice, mustard, curry, salt, onion, sugar, and sour cream. Add gelatin and mix well. Chill until slightly thickened.

---

* Two teaspoons curry is a mild flavoring. Taste for seasoning, and if you desire, add more.

Add the chicken and celery. Chop the apples (including skin) directly into the mixture. Mix well. Turn into the prepared mold and chill until set.

Unmold, using Method 3.

CHICKEN MOUSSE
(5-cup mold, lightly oiled)

    1 envelope unflavored gelatin
    1½ cups chicken broth, divided
    3 egg yolks, lightly beaten
    1 tablespoon lemon juice
    ¼ teaspoon salt
    ⅛ teaspoon pepper
    1 teaspoon celery seed
    ½ cup mayonnaise
    1½ cups finely ground cooked chicken
    1 cup heavy cream, whipped

Soften the gelatin in ¾ cup of chicken broth for 5 minutes. In a small saucepan, combine egg yolks with the remaining chicken broth, lemon juice, salt, and pepper. Stir constantly over low heat until the mixture thickens slightly. (Do not boil.) Add the softened gelatin and stir until gelatin is dissolved. Remove from heat and cool slightly.

Add the celery seed and mayonnaise. Chill until slightly thickened.

Fold in the chicken and whipped cream. Turn into the prepared mold and chill until set.

Unmold, using Method 3.

LEMON CHICKEN-AND-ZUCCHINI MOUSSE
(8-cup mold, lightly oiled)

    2 envelopes unflavored gelatin
    1½ cups chicken broth, divided
    1 cup sour cream
    1 teaspoon salt
    ⅛ teaspoon pepper
    1 tablespoon lemon juice
    Grated rind of 1 lemon
    1 tablespoon grated onion
    2½ cups finely chopped cooked chicken
    2 medium zucchini, washed, peeled in strips, and chopped
        raw
    2 cups heavy cream, whipped

Sprinkle gelatin over 1 cup chicken broth in a small saucepan and let stand for 5 minutes to soften. Stir constantly over low heat until gelatin is dissolved, about 5 minutes. Turn off heat and set aside to cool.

In a mixing bowl, combine remaining ½ cup chicken broth, sour cream, salt, pepper, lemon juice, rind, and onion. Add dissolved gelatin. Chill, stirring occasionally, until slightly thickened.

Stir in chicken and zucchini. Fold in the whipped cream. Turn into the prepared mold and chill until set.

Unmold, using Method 3.

TARRAGON CHICKEN MOUSSE
(5-cup mold, lightly oiled)

> 1 envelope plus 1½ teaspoons unflavored gelatin
> ½ cup cold water
> 1 tablespoon cognac or applejack
> 2 chicken breasts, skinned and boned
> ½ cup dry white wine
> 1 teaspoon chopped fresh tarragon or ½ teaspoon dried
>   tarragon
> 2 teaspoons finely chopped shallots
> 1 can (10¾ ounces) chicken broth
> ½ teaspoon salt
> ¼ teaspoon white pepper
> 1 cup heavy cream, whipped

Soften the gelatin in the water combined with the cognac. Place the chicken breasts in a bowl with the white wine, tarragon, and shallots. Cover and refrigerate for ½ hour. Place the chicken mixture in a saucepan and add the chicken broth, salt, and pepper. Bring to a boil; cover and simmer gently until the chicken is cooked through, about 20 minutes. Remove chicken from broth and set aside to cool slightly. Add the softened gelatin to the hot broth and stir until gelatin is dissolved. Chill until slightly thickened, stirring occasionally.

Put the chicken through the coarse plate of a meat grinder. Beat the thickened gelatin mixture until smooth. Add the ground chicken. Fold in the whipped cream. Turn into the prepared mold and chill until set.

Unmold, using Method 3.

MOLDED CORNED BEEF SALAD
(6-cup mold, lightly oiled)

2 tablespoons vinegar
½ teaspoon salt
½ teaspoon sugar
⅛ teaspoon pepper
1 teaspoon chopped parsley
1 teaspoon snipped chives
1 cup diced cooked potatoes
2 hard-cooked eggs, chopped
1 envelope unflavored gelatin
1 cup tomato juice
1½ cups mayonnaise
½ cup sour cream
1 cup chopped cooked corned beef

Combine the vinegar, salt, sugar, pepper, and herbs. Mix with the potatoes and eggs. Cover and marinate in the refrigerator for 1 hour.

Sprinkle the gelatin over the tomato juice in a small saucepan and let stand for 5 minutes to soften. Place over low heat, stirring constantly, until gelatin is dissolved. Cool.

Stir in the mayonnaise and sour cream. Chill until slightly thickened.

Add the corned beef to the chilled gelatin. Add the potato salad. Turn into the prepared mold and chill until set.

Unmold, using Method 3.

LAYERED DUCK WITH CHERRIES IN ASPIC
(6-cup mold, dipped in cold water)

4 cups Basic Aspic (page 136)
1 pound Bing cherries, halved and pitted
2 cups thinly sliced cooked duck
Salt and pepper to taste

Make Basic Aspic with seasoned stock made from the duck carcass. Pour a thin layer of aspic into the prepared mold and chill until very thick. At the same time, place the remaining aspic in the refrigerator so that it can start its chilling process to become the consistency of thick syrup. It will be quicker and easier to work with when layering. (See Tips on Layering, pages 15–16.)

Using the cherry halves (rounded side down), arrange a design on top of the firm aspic in the mold. Carefully spoon another layer of syrupy aspic over the cherries to set the pattern. Chill.

Add a layer of sliced duck, sprinkled with salt and pepper, then aspic. Chill.

Continue layering and chilling, alternating with cherries-aspic, duck-aspic, until the mold is full. Chill until set. Also chill any leftover aspic in a cup or other container until set.

Unmold Layered Duck, using Method 1 or 2. Unmold leftover aspic, using Method 1 or 2. Chop* the aspic and use as a garnish around the Layered Duck.

Variations

LAYERED DUCK WITH APRICOTS

When making the Basic Aspic, substitute 2 tablespoons of apricot-flavored brandy for the 2 tablespoons of port called for in the recipe.

---

* See notes on Leftover Aspic, page 127.

Substitute 1 can (17 ounces) whole peeled apricots, cut in half, for the 1 pound of cherries.

LAYERED DUCK WITH ORANGES

When making the Basic Aspic, substitute 2 tablespoons of orange-flavored liqueur for the 2 tablespoons of port called for in the recipe.

Substitute 4 large navel oranges, peeled and sectioned, for the 1 pound of cherries.

DUCK MOUSSE WITH PEACHES IN ASPIC
(6-cup mold, dipped in cold water)

> 4 cups Basic Aspic (page 136), using 3 tablespoons orange-flavored liqueur for the port and cognac in the recipe
> 1 can (8 ounces) sliced peaches, drained (reserve liquid)
> ¼ cup orange-flavored liqueur
> 1 teaspoon unflavored gelatin
> 1 tablespoon butter
> 3 tablespoons finely chopped onion
> 1 tablespoon flour
> 1 cup milk
> Salt and pepper to taste
> 2 cups finely chopped or ground cooked duck
> 1 cup heavy cream, whipped
> 1 can (17 ounces) peach halves (for garnish)

Make Basic Aspic with seasoned stock made from the duck carcass. Pour a thin layer of the aspic in the bottom of the prepared mold and chill until very thick.

Using the sliced peaches, arrange a design on top of the chilled aspic in the mold. Carefully spoon another layer of aspic over the peaches to set the pattern. Chill.

Combine the ¼ cup liqueur and the reserved peach liquid. Sprinkle the gelatin on the combined liquids and let stand to soften.

Melt the butter in a medium-sized saucepan. Add the chopped onion and stir until onion is limp and transparent. Add the flour; stir. Gradually add the milk, stirring constantly until mixture begins to thicken. Stir in 2 cups of Basic Aspic. Remove from heat. Add the softened gelatin to the warm mixture, stirring until gelatin is dissolved. Add salt and pepper to taste. Chill until slightly thickened, stirring occasionally.

Add chopped duck. Fold in the whipped cream. Turn into the prepared mold with the set design. Chill until set. Also chill any leftover aspic in a cup or other container until set.

Unmold Duck Mousse, using Method 1 or 2. Unmold leftover aspic, using Method 1 or 2. Chop* the aspic and use as a garnish around the mousse with the peach halves.

PORTED GOOSE MOUSSE WITH APPLES IN ASPIC
(6-cup mold, dipped in cold water)

4 cups Basic Aspic (page 136)
2 Delicious (red) apples, cored
1 teaspoon unflavored gelatin
2 tablespoons port wine
1 tablespoon butter
3 tablespoons finely chopped onion
1 tablespoon flour
1 cup milk
Salt and pepper to taste
2 cups finely chopped or ground cooked goose
1 cup heavy cream, whipped

* See notes on Leftover Aspic, page 127.

Make Basic Aspic with seasoned stock made from the goose carcass. Pour a thin layer in the bottom of the prepared mold and chill until very thick.

Slice one apple with skin and arrange a design on top of the chilled aspic in the mold. Carefully spoon another thin layer of aspic over the apple slices to set the pattern. Chill.

Soften the gelatin in the port wine. Melt the butter in a medium-sized saucepan. Add the chopped onion and stir until onion is limp and transparent. Add the flour; stir. Gradually add the milk, stirring constantly until mixture begins to thicken. Stir in 2 cups of Basic Aspic. Remove from heat. Add the softened gelatin to the warm mixture, stirring until gelatin is dissolved. Add salt and pepper to taste. Using large hole of grater, grate the remaining apple with skin directly into the warm sauce. Chill sauce until slightly thickened, stirring occasionally.

Add chopped goose. Fold in the whipped cream. Turn into the prepared mold with the set design. Chill until set. Also chill any leftover aspic in a cup or other container until set.

Unmold Goose Mousse, using Method 1 or 2. Unmold leftover aspic, using Method 1 or 2. Chop* the aspic and use as a garnish around the mousse.

HAM WITH APPLES IN ASPIC
(4-cup mold, dipped in cold water)

4 cups Basic Aspic (page 136)
3 Delicious (red) apples
¾ pound cooked ham, sliced thin with fat removed

Make Basic Aspic with seasoned stock made from chicken or veal. Chill until the consistency of thick syrup. (See Tips on Layering, pages 15–16.)

* See notes on Leftover Aspic, page 127.

Pour a thin layer of aspic into the prepared mold and chill until very thick.

Slice one apple with skin and arrange a design on top of the chilled aspic in the mold. Carefully spoon another layer of syrupy aspic over the apples to set the pattern. Chill until very thick.

About 1/4 to 1/2 inch from the edge of the mold, arrange several slices of ham around the center. Cover with syrupy aspic and chill until very thick.

Using large hole of grater, grate a layer of apple with skin directly into the mold to within 1/4 to 1/2 inch of the rim. Cover with syrupy aspic and chill until very thick.

Continue alternating layers of ham-aspic and grated apple-aspic until the mold is full. Chill until set. Also chill any left-over aspic in a cup or other container until set.

Unmold Ham with Apples, using Method 1 or 2. Unmold leftover aspic, using Method 1 or 2. Chop* the aspic and use as a garnish.

HAM-AND-CHEESE MOUSSE
(6-cup mold, lightly oiled)

   2 tablespoons butter
   2 tablespoons flour
   1/2 cup chicken broth
   1/2 cup heavy cream
   2 triangles Gruyère cheese
   2 tablespoons grated Parmesan
   1 tablespoon grated onion
   1/4 teaspoon cayenne pepper
   1 envelope unflavored gelatin
   1/4 cup cold water
   1/4 cup mayonnaise

* See notes on Leftover Aspic, page 127.

¼ cup chopped green pepper
1 cup cooked elbow macaroni
2 cups finely chopped ham
½ cup heavy cream, whipped

In a medium-sized saucepan, melt the butter and add the flour, stirring until smooth. Remove from heat. Gradually add the chicken broth and heavy cream. Return to low heat and cook, stirring constantly until the mixture begins to thicken. Add the cheeses, onion, and cayenne, stirring until smooth. (Do not boil.) Remove from heat.

Soften the gelatin in the cold water. Add to the hot sauce, stirring until gelatin is dissolved. Set aside to cool, stirring occasionally.

Add the mayonnaise and chill until slightly thickened.

Add the green pepper, macaroni, and ham. Mix well. Fold in the whipped cream. Turn into the prepared mold and chill until set.

Unmold, using Method 3.

HAM-AND-CIDER MOUSSE
(5-cup mold, lightly oiled)

1 envelope unflavored gelatin
1¼ cups apple cider, divided
½ cup mayonnaise
1 teaspoon grated lemon rind
2 cups diced cooked ham
1 small Delicious (red) apple, cored
½ cup heavy cream, whipped

In a small heat-resistant cup, soften the gelatin in ¼ cup of cider. Place cup in hot water over low heat, stirring until

gelatin is dissolved. Add to the remaining 1 cup cider. Stir in
the mayonnaise and lemon rind. Chill until slightly thickened.

Add the ham. Finely dice the apple with skin directly into
the mixture. Fold in the whipped cream. Turn into the prepared mold and chill until set.

Unmold, using Method 3.

HAM MOUSSE
(4-cup mold, lightly oiled)

    1 envelope unflavored gelatin
    1 cup cold chicken broth, fat removed
    1 tablespoon sherry
    ½ cup mayonnaise
    1½ cups ground or finely chopped cooked ham
    1 stalk celery, grated
    1 teaspoon prepared mustard
    ½ cup heavy cream, whipped

In a small saucepan, sprinkle the gelatin over the chicken
broth and let stand 5 minutes to soften. Place over low heat,
stirring until gelatin is dissolved. Remove from heat. Add the
sherry. Cool.

Stir in the mayonnaise. Chill until slightly thickened, stirring occasionally.

Combine the ham, celery, and mustard. Stir into the
chilled gelatin. Fold in the whipped cream. Turn into the
prepared mold and chill until set.

Unmold, using Method 3.

BRANDIED MEAT LOAF ASPIC

(5-cup mold, dipped in cold water)

    1 envelope plus 1 teaspoon unflavored gelatin
    ½ cup cold water
    2 cups seasoned beef consommé
    1 tablespoon brandy
    2 hard-cooked eggs, peeled and sliced
    2 cups finely diced cooked beef, fat removed
    ½ cup finely chopped celery
    1 small green bell pepper, finely chopped
    1 tablespoon minced onion
    2 tablespoons chopped parsley

In a small heat-resistant cup, sprinkle the gelatin over the water and let stand for 5 minutes to soften. Place cup in a pan of hot water over low heat, stirring until gelatin is dissolved. Add to the consommé. Stir in the brandy. Chill slightly.

Pour a thin layer into the bottom of the mold and chill until set but not too firm.

Using the sliced hard-cooked eggs, arrange a design in the mold on top of the set gelatin. Slightly overlap the slices, if necessary. Ladle another thin layer of gelatin over the design and chill to set the pattern. Chill the remaining gelatin until slightly thickened.

Combine the remaining ingredients and fold into the thickened gelatin. Turn into the patterned mold and chill until set.

Unmold, using Method 1 or 2.

JELLIED PIGS KNUCKLES
(6-cup mold, dipped in cold water)

4 pigs knuckles
6 cups water
1/3 cup vinegar
1 tablespoon salt
2 bay leaves
6 peppercorns
1 carrot, diced
½ teaspoon celery seed
1 onion, studded with 2 cloves
2 cloves garlic
Pepper
¼ cup finely chopped parsley
⅛ teaspoon sugar
1 envelope unflavored gelatin
¼ cup dry white wine
1 teaspoon minced fresh dill
¼ pound cooked tongue, chopped
1 tablespoon small capers

Wash pigs knuckles and place in a large pan with water, vinegar, salt, bay leaves, peppercorns, carrot, celery seed, onion, and garlic. Bring to a boil; cover and simmer on low heat for about 2½ hours, or until meat falls away from the bones.

Remove pigs knuckles from stock. Remove meat from the bones and chop into small pieces. Sprinkle with pepper and parsley. Set aside.

Strain broth and skim off fat. Add sugar and cook for another 15 minutes. Remove from heat.

Soften gelatin in the wine for 5 minutes. Add to stock, stirring until gelatin is dissolved. Chill until slightly thickened, stirring occasionally

Add dill, tongue, and capers, mixing well. Add knuckle meat. Turn into the prepared mold and chill until set.

Unmold, using Method 1 or 2.

ROQUEFORT CHEF SALAD MOUSSE
(5-cup mold, lightly oiled)

1 envelope plus 1 teaspoon unflavored gelatin
1 cup cold milk
2 ounces Roquefort or blue cheese, crumbled
1 tablespoon lemon juice
1 tablespoon white wine vinegar
1 tablespoon grated onion
1 clove garlic, crushed
1/4 teaspoon salt
1/8 teaspoon white pepper
1/4 cup mayonnaise
1 cup sour cream
2/3 cup finely chopped boiled ham
2/3 cup finely chopped chicken or turkey meat
1/2 cup finely chopped green bell pepper
1/2 cup finely chopped Swiss cheese
2 tomatoes, peeled, seeded, and diced
1 hard-cooked egg, peeled and chopped

In a small saucepan, sprinkle the gelatin over the milk and let stand 5 minutes to soften. Place over low heat, stirring until gelatin is dissolved. (Do not boil.) Remove from heat. Add the Roquefort and beat until blended. Cool slightly.

Stir in the lemon juice, vinegar, onion, garlic, salt, pepper, mayonnaise, and sour cream. Chill until slightly thickened, stirring occasionally.

Fold in the remaining ingredients. Turn into the prepared mold and chill until set.

Unmold, using Method 3.

Serve on salad greens.

JELLIED TONGUE RING
(4-cup ring mold, dipped in cold water)

3 tablespoons sherry
3 tablespoons cold water
1 envelope unflavored gelatin
1 can (13 ounces) beef consommé
5 stuffed olives, sliced
1 teaspoon small capers
6 tiny sweet pickles, sliced
2 cups chopped cooked tongue

In a small heat-resistant bowl, combine the sherry and water. Sprinkle the gelatin into the bowl and let stand 5 minutes to soften. Place bowl in a pan of hot (not boiling) water over low heat, stirring until gelatin is dissolved. Add to the beef consommé, mixing well. Pour a thin layer into the prepared mold and chill until thick. Chill the remaining gelatin until it is the consistency of a thick syrup.

Arrange the olives, capers, and sliced pickles in a design on top of the set aspic in the mold. Carefully spoon a layer of the syrupy gelatin over the design to set the pattern. Chill until very thick.

Fold the tongue into the syrupy gelatin. When the pattern in the mold has nearly set, add the tongue mixture and chill until completely set.

Unmold, using Method 1 or 2.

Fill the ring with potato salad.

TURKEY-CRANBERRY MOUSSE
(8-cup mold, lightly oiled)

TURKEY LAYER

   3 egg yolks
   1 envelope unflavored gelatin
   1/4 teaspoon nutmeg
   1/4 teaspoon salt
   1/8 teaspoon pepper
   1 1/2 cups chicken or turkey broth
   2 tablespoons sherry
   1/2 cup mayonnaise
   2 cups finely chopped cooked turkey
   1/2 cup heavy cream, whipped

CRANBERRY LAYER

   1 envelope unflavored gelatin
   1/4 cup orange juice
   1 can (1 pound) whole cranberry sauce
   1 tablespoon grated orange rind

TURKEY LAYER

In a medium-sized saucepan, lightly beat the egg yolks with the gelatin, nutmeg, salt, and pepper. Gradually add the broth, stirring constantly over low heat until the mixture begins to thicken. Turn off heat. Cool slightly.

Add the sherry and mayonnaise. Chill until slightly thickened, stirring occasionally.

Add the turkey, mixing well. Fold in the whipped cream. Turn into the prepared mold and chill until almost set. (See Tips on Layering, pages 15–16.)

CRANBERRY LAYER

In a small heat-resistant cup, sprinkle the gelatin over the orange juice. Place in a pan of hot (not boiling) water over low heat, stirring until dissolved. Add to the cranberry sauce. Stir in the orange rind. Chill until slightly thickened.

Turn into the mold, carefully pouring on top of the nearly set turkey mousse. Chill until completely set.

Unmold, using Method 3.

MOLDED VEAL SALAD
(6-cup mold, lightly oiled)

¼ cup vinegar
2 tablespoons mixed chopped herbs (tarragon, parsley, chives, basil)
1 teaspoon salt
1 teaspoon sugar
¼ teaspoon pepper
½ teaspoon paprika
1 small clove garlic, crushed
1½ cups chopped cooked veal
1 cup diced cooked potatoes
1/3 cup pitted and chopped ripe olives
1 envelope plus 1 teaspoon unflavored gelatin
1¼ cups tomato juice
1 cup mayonnaise
1 cup sour cream

Combine the vinegar, herbs, salt, sugar, pepper, paprika, and garlic. Pour over the veal, potatoes, and olives. Cover and marinate in the refrigerator for 1 hour.

In a small saucepan, sprinkle the gelatin over the tomato juice and let stand for 5 minutes to soften. Place over low heat, stirring until gelatin is dissolved. Cool slightly.

Add the mayonnaise and sour cream. Chill until slightly thickened, stirring occasionally.

Fold in the seasoned meat-and-potato mixture, mixing well. Taste for seasoning. Turn into the prepared mold and chill until set.

Unmold, using Method 3.

VEAL AND OLIVES IN WINE ASPIC
(4-cup mold, dipped in cold water)

1 envelope plus 1 teaspoon unflavored gelatin
1/3 cup dry white wine
1-2/3 cups veal or chicken stock, seasoned
2 hard-cooked eggs (1 sliced, 1 chopped)
10 jumbo ripe olives, pitted and sliced
½ cup tomato juice
1½ cups finely chopped cooked veal
2 tablespoons minced parsley
2 teaspoons minced onion

In a small heat-resistant cup, soften the gelatin in the wine for 5 minutes. Place cup in a pan of hot water over low heat, stirring until gelatin is dissolved. Add to the stock, mixing well. Chill slightly.

Pour a very thin layer into the bottom of the mold and chill until set. Using the sliced egg and a few olives, arrange a design in the mold on top of the set gelatin. Ladle another thin layer of gelatin over the design and chill to set the pattern.

Add the tomato juice to the remaining gelatin and chill until slightly thickened.

Combine the chopped egg and remaining olive slices with the veal, parsley, and onion. Fold into the thickened gelatin. Turn into the patterned mold and chill until set.

Unmold, using Method 1 or 2.

VIENNA POTATO SALAD
(8-cup mold, lightly oiled)

> 1 envelope unflavored gelatin
> ¼ cup lemon juice
> 1 cup water
> 1 teaspoon sugar
> 1 teaspoon salt
> ¼ teaspoon pepper
> 3 cups diced cooked potatoes
> 2 hard-cooked eggs, peeled and chopped
> 1 red apple
> ¼ cup chopped green pepper
> 2 tablespoons grated onion
> 3 cans (4 ounces each) Vienna sausages, drained and cubed
> 1 cup mayonnaise
> ½ cup heavy cream, whipped

In a small heat-resistant cup, sprinkle the gelatin over the lemon juice and let stand for 5 minutes to soften. Place cup in a pan of hot water over low heat, stirring until gelatin is dissolved. Combine the water, sugar, and salt. Add the dissolved gelatin. Cool.

Combine the remaining ingredients, except for the whipped cream, in a mixing bowl, chopping the apple directly into the mixture to prevent it from discoloring. Add the cooled gelatin mixture to the potato mixture. Fold in the whipped cream. Turn into the prepared mold and chill until set.

Unmold, using Method 3.

CLAM MOUSSE
(6-cup mold, lightly oiled)

1 envelope unflavored gelatin
1 cup clam juice, divided
1/4 cup white wine
1/2 cup mayonnaise
18 cherrystone clams, steamed open
1 tablespoon chopped chives
1 tablespoon chopped parsley
1 carrot, peeled and grated
1 stalk celery, grated
1 teaspoon grated lemon rind
1/2 teaspoon salt
1/4 teaspoon white pepper
1 cup heavy cream, whipped

In a small heat-resistant cup, sprinkle the gelatin over 1/4 cup of clam juice and let stand 5 minutes to soften. Place cup in a pan of hot water over low heat, stirring until gelatin is dissolved. Combine the remaining clam juice, white wine, and mayonnaise. Add the dissolved gelatin. Chill until slightly thickened.

Chop the clams. Combine with the chives, parsley, carrot, celery, lemon rind, salt, and pepper. Add to the slightly thickened gelatin mixture. Fold in the whipped cream. Turn into the prepared mold and chill until set.

Unmold, using Method 3. Use clam shells for decoration around plate.

CRAB MEAT IN AVOCADO MOUSSE LAYERED WITH TOMATO ASPIC

(6-cup loaf pan or mold, lightly oiled)

CRABMEAT IN AVOCADO MOUSSE

2 envelopes unflavored gelatin
1½ cups cold milk, divided
1 pint sour cream
¼ cup lemon juice
½ teaspoon hot pepper sauce
1 teaspoon salt
2 mashed ripe avocados
½ cup minced celery
1 can (6–7 ounces) crab meat, drained and flaked

In a small heat-resistant cup, sprinkle the gelatin over ½ cup cold milk and let stand 5 minutes to soften. Place in a pan of hot water, over low heat, gently stirring until dissolved.

Combine the remaining milk, sour cream, lemon juice, pepper sauce, salt and avocados in a large bowl and blend well with a rotary mixer; add the dissolved gelatin. Chill until slightly thickened. Fold in the celery and crab meat. Turn into the prepared mold and chill until firm, but not set.

TOMATO ASPIC

1 envelope plus 1 teaspoon unflavored gelatin
2 cups tomato juice, divided

In a small heat-resistant cup, sprinkle the gelatin over ½ cup tomato juice and let stand for 5 minutes to soften. Place in a pan of hot water, over low heat, gently stirring until dissolved. Add to the remaining tomato juice, mixing well. Chill until slightly thickened. Gently pour into the mold on top of the firm avocado mousse. Chill until set.

Unmold, using Method 3. Garnish with sliced avocado brushed with lemon juice.

MOLDED CRAB MEAT SALAD
(2½-cup mold, lightly oiled)

    2 teaspoons unflavored gelatin
    ¼ cup cold water
    2 tablespoons lemon juice
    ¾ cup mayonnaise
    12 ounces cooked crab meat, picked over
    1 tablespoon grated onion
    Dash hot pepper sauce
    2 tablespoons finely minced celery

Sprinkle the gelatin over the cold water and lemon juice in a small heat-resistant cup and let stand for 5 minutes to soften. Place cup in a pan of hot water over low heat, stirring until gelatin is dissolved. Combine the remaining ingredients and add the dissolved gelatin. Turn into the prepared mold and chill until set.

Unmold, using Method 3.

EEL-AND-EGG ASPIC
(7-cup mold, dipped in cold water)

2 envelopes unflavored gelatin
1/3 cup cold water
1/3 cup dry white wine
2 cups chicken broth (fat removed), divided
1 cup fish stock, strained (liquid used to cook eel)
3 hard-cooked eggs (1 sliced, 2 chopped)
¾ cup mayonnaise
2 tablespoons fresh chopped dill or 2 teaspoons dried dill
1 stalk celery, minced
2 cups cooked eel, skinned, boned, and flaked

Soften the gelatin in the combined cold water and wine. Bring ½ cup of broth to a boil. Remove from heat. Stir in the softened gelatin, until gelatin is dissolved. (Reheat, if necessary.) Add to the remaining 1½ cups chicken broth and the fish stock. Chill until slightly thickened, but still loose enough to pour.

Pour a thin layer of gelatin into the bottom of the mold. Chill until set.

Using the sliced egg, arrange a pattern on top of the set gelatin in the mold. Ladle another layer of cold gelatin over the eggs and chill to set the pattern. Return the remaining gelatin to the refrigerator to chill until slightly thicker (a mound will form when dropped from a spoon).

Whisk the mayonnaise into the thickened gelatin until smooth. Taste for seasoning.

Combine the chopped eggs, dill, celery, and eel. Toss lightly. Fold into the gelatin mixture. Turn into the patterned mold and chill until set.

Unmold, using Method 1 or 2.

FRESH FISH MOUSSE
(4-cup mold, lightly oiled)

1 envelope unflavored gelatin
½ cup cold water
½ cup fresh lemon or lime juice
2 tablespoons sugar
2 teaspoons dry mustard
2 teaspoons salt
¼ teaspoon white pepper
½ cup sour cream
2 cups flaked cooked fish
¼ cup snipped fresh dill
½ cup heavy cream, whipped

In a small heat-resistant cup, sprinkle the gelatin over the cold water and let stand 5 minutes to soften. Place cup in a pan of hot water over low heat, stirring until gelatin is dissolved.

In a mixing bowl, combine the juice, sugar, mustard, salt, pepper, and sour cream. Add the dissolved gelatin and beat until well blended. Chill until slightly thickened.

Fold in the fish and dill. Fold in the whipped cream. Turn into the prepared mold and chill until set.

Unmold, using Method 3.

HADDOCK MOUSSE
(6-cup mold, lightly oiled)

2 tablespoons butter
1 tablespoon finely minced onion
1/4 teaspoon nutmeg
1 teaspoon paprika
4 teaspoons flour
1/2 cup clam juice
1 cup milk, scalded
Salt and pepper to taste
1 envelope unflavored gelatin
1/4 cup white wine
2 tablespoons sherry
1 pound haddock fillet, cooked and flaked
1 cup heavy cream, whipped

Melt the butter in a medium-sized saucepan. Add the onion and cook over low heat until onion is transparent. Add the nutmeg, paprika, and flour, stirring to make a roux. Remove from heat. Stir in the clam juice until smooth. Return to low heat. Add the milk, stirring constantly until the mixture thickens. Remove from heat. Add salt and pepper to taste.

Sprinkle the gelatin over the combined wine and sherry. Let stand for 5 minutes to soften. Stir into the hot sauce until gelatin is dissolved. Chill until slightly thickened, stirring occasionally.

Add the flaked fish. Fold in the whipped cream. Turn into the prepared mold and chill until set.

Unmold, using Method 3.

HERRING SALAD RING
(6-cup ring mold, lightly oiled)

1 envelope unflavored gelatin
1/4 cup cold water
1 tablespoon lemon juice
1 jar (8 ounces) herring fillets (in sour cream or wine sauce)
1 hard-cooked egg, peeled and chopped
1/2 cup diced pickled beets
1/4 cup finely chopped onion
1/4 cup finely chopped dill pickles
3/4 cup diced boiled potatoes
1/2 cup diced apples
1 tablespoon capers
1/2 cup mayonnaise
1/2 teaspoon prepared mustard
1 cup sour cream

Sprinkle the gelatin over the water and lemon juice in a small heat-resistant cup and let stand for 5 minutes to soften. Place cup in a pan of hot water, stirring until gelatin is dissolved.

Chop the herring fillets into small pieces. Combine them and their juice with the remaining ingredients. Add the dissolved gelatin and mix well. Turn into the prepared mold and chill until set.

Unmold, using Method 3.

LOBSTER MOUSSE
(6-cup mold, lightly oiled)

1 envelope unflavored gelatin
1/4 cup dry white wine
2 1/2-pound lobster, steamed or boiled
1 tablespoon butter
1 tablespoon flour
1 teaspoon paprika
1 cup chicken broth
Salt to taste
1 cup mayonnaise
1/2 cup heavy cream, whipped

Sprinkle the gelatin over the white wine to soften. Remove the meat from the cooked lobster. Chop, cover, and chill.

In a small saucepan, melt the butter. Add the flour and paprika, stirring to make a roux. Remove from heat. Gradually add the chicken broth, stirring until smooth. Return to low heat and cook, stirring constantly, until mixture begins to thicken slightly. Add the softened gelatin, stirring until gelatin is dissolved. Remove from heat. Add salt to taste. Cool slightly.

Stir into the mayonnaise in a large mixing bowl. Chill until slightly thickened.

Add the lobster meat, mixing well. Fold in the whipped cream. Turn into the prepared mold and chill until set.

Unmold, using Method 3.

MUSSEL CHOWDER MOUSSE
(8-cup mold, lightly oiled)

2 pounds mussels, cleaned
4 cups water

3 tablespoons bacon fat
1 green bell pepper, chopped
1 onion, chopped
1 stalk celery, chopped
2 medium potatoes, peeled and diced
1 bay leaf
2 envelopes plus 1 teaspoon unflavored gelatin
1½ cups milk, divided
Salt and white pepper
2 tablespoons chopped parsley
1 cup heavy cream, whipped

Cover and steam open the mussels in the water. Do not over-cook. Set aside to cool in the liquid.

In a medium-sized saucepan, melt the bacon fat. Add the green pepper, onion, and celery. Gently sauté until the onion is transparent.

From the top of the mussel broth, measure out 2 cups of liquid. Strain through 3 layers of cheesecloth. Add the strained broth to the pan of sautéed vegetables. Add the potatoes and bay leaf. Bring to a boil; cover and simmer about 25 minutes, or until the potatoes are tender. Remove the bay leaf. Place the mixture in a blender, a small amount at a time, to purée.

Soften the gelatin in ½ cup milk for 5 minutes. Add to the hot purée and stir until gelatin is dissolved (or process in the blender with some of the purée). Transfer to a large mixing bowl. Use the remaining 1 cup of milk to rinse out the blender, and pour into the purée. Taste for seasoning. Add salt and white pepper to taste. Chill until cool and slightly thickened, stirring occasionally.

Return to the mussels, which are still cooling in the remaining 2 cups of broth. Remove the mussels from their shells and gently swish them (one at a time) through the remaining liquid to remove any grit. Chop the cleaned mussels. Sprinkle with parsley.

Whisk the thickened gelatin to remove all lumps. Stir in the mussels. Fold in the whipped cream. Turn into the prepared mold and chill until set.

Unmold, using Method 3.

MUSSELS MARINIÈRE ASPIC
(4-cup mold, dipped in cold water)

  1½ pounds fresh mussels, cleaned
  1 onion, quartered
  1 carrot, quartered
  1 celery stalk, quartered
  3 cloves garlic, peeled
  2 bay leaves
  ¾ cup dry white wine
  ¾ cup water
  1 envelope unflavored gelatin
  ½ cup tomato juice
  2 tablespoons chopped parsley
  ⅛ teaspoon cayenne pepper
  Salt (optional)

In a large soup pan, combine the mussels with the onion, carrot, celery, garlic, and bay leaves. Add the white wine and water. Cover the pan and cook over medium heat about 7 minutes, or until the shells open. Remove from heat and let stand to cool slightly.

Soften the gelatin in the tomato juice.

Using a slotted spoon, remove mussels from broth. Discard the shells, or reserve for garnish around the platter. If mussels are large, cut in half, otherwise leave whole. Sprinkle with parsley and set aside.

Strain the broth through 3 thicknesses of cheesecloth into a mixing bowl. Add the softened gelatin and stir until gelatin is dissolved. (The broth should still be hot enough. If not, reheat.) Add the cayenne and taste for seasoning. Add salt, if desired. Chill until slightly thickened, stirring occasionally.

Lightly whisk the thickened gelatin until smooth. Stir in the mussels. Turn into the prepared mold and chill until set.

Unmold, using Method 1 or 2.

OCTOPUS IN ASPIC
(8-cup mold, dipped in cold water)

1 octopus (3 pounds)*
Juice of 1 lemon
¾ cup chopped celery
¾ cup chopped pimiento
¼ cup small capers
1 recipe No-Stock Fish Aspic (page 137)†

Place the octopus in a large pan of cold water. Bring to a boil and cook for 20 minutes. Change the water, return to a boil, and cook for 30 minutes. Repeat this step two or three times. The octopus will be cooked when the water boils clear.

Rinse the cooked octopus in cold water. Return it to the pan and cover with cold water. The cleaning process is easiest done underwater. Grasp the head of the octopus in one

---

* When buying the octopus, be sure to purchase only one weighing 3 pounds, rather than two or three smaller ones. The smaller ones do not contain as much usable meat. It is also very likely that the octopus will be frozen. Advise your fish market that you want one 3-pound *defrosted* octopus, so that you do not pay for part of the weight in ice.

† When making the No-Stock Fish Aspic for use in this recipe, boil down to 3¼ cups rather than to 2½ cups. Add the remaining ½ cup of white wine, so that you are finally left with 3¾ cups of aspic.

hand. Using the thumb and forefinger of the other hand, gently encircle one tentacle at the base of the head. Slide this hand down the length of the tentacle to remove the skin and suckers. Discard all the skin that floats away, so that you are left with a tentacle of pure white meat. Gently tear the tentacle off the head and set tentacle aside. Repeat this process with each tentacle, finally discarding the head. Rinse the cleaned tentacles in cold water. Chop into ½-inch slices. (This may seem a very tedious way to prepare the octopus, but the end result is a tender, succulent treat.)

Measure out 2½ cups of chopped octopus. (If there is extra, sprinkle it with lemon juice and indulge yourself.) Mix the chopped octopus in a bowl with the lemon juice, celery, pimiento, and capers. Cover and refrigerate for 1 hour or longer.

Chill the aspic until slightly thickened. Stir in the octopus salad. Turn into the prepared mold and chill until set.

Unmold, using Method 1 or 2.

Variation

SCALLOPS IN ASPIC

Omit the octopus and substitute 2½ cups of cooked scallops. To cook the scallops, simmer them in white wine for 5 or 6 minutes.

FRESH OYSTER MOUSSE
(6-cup mold, lightly oiled)

    1 envelope plus 1½ teaspoons unflavored gelatin
    ⅓ cup dry white wine
    1 tablespoon butter
    ¼ cup finely chopped onion
    1 cup milk
    1 cup clam juice
    1 pint shucked fresh oysters with their liquor
    Salt and white pepper to taste
    1 cup heavy cream, whipped

Soften the gelatin in the wine. Melt the butter in a medium-sized saucepan. Add the onion and cook until onion is transparent. Add the milk and clam juice and bring to a boil. Add the oysters. Turn heat to very low and simmer for about 5 minutes, or until edges of oysters curl. Remove from heat. Add the softened gelatin to the hot mixture and stir until gelatin is dissolved. Add salt and pepper to taste. Adding a small amount at a time, purée all the mixture with oysters in a blender until smooth. Pour into a bowl and chill until slightly thickened, stirring occasionally.

    Fold in the whipped cream. Turn into the prepared mold and chill until set.

    Unmold, using Method 3.

DOYLE'S SALMON MOUSSE
(4-cup mold, lightly oiled)

1 envelope unflavored gelatin
½ cup boiling water
2 tablespoons lemon juice
1 thin slice of onion
¼ cup mayonnaise
¼ cup sour cream
1 pound fresh salmon, drained and flaked after steaming
about 3 or 4 minutes
¼ teaspoon paprika
1 teaspoon chopped fresh dill
1 cup heavy cream
1 cucumber, sliced (for garnish)
Watercress (for garnish)

In a blender, combine gelatin, boiling water, lemon juice, and onion. Cover and blend on high speed for 40 seconds. Add the mayonnaise, sour cream, salmon, paprika, and dill. Cover and blend on high speed until smooth and creamy. Add the heavy cream. Blend 30 seconds. Cream may curdle if blended too long. Turn into the prepared mold and chill until set.

Unmold, using Method 3. Garnish with cucumber slices and watercress.

Serve with Dilled Caper Sauce (below).

DILLED CAPER SAUCE
(Yield: 1 cup)

½ cup mayonnaise
½ cup sour cream
2 tablespoons lemon juice

1 tablespoon finely chopped fresh dill or 1½ teaspoons
   dried dillweed
1 tablespoon minced capers
½ teaspoon salt
½ teaspoon sugar
Pinch pepper

Combine all ingredients in a small bowl; whisk until smooth.
Refrigerate covered.

MOLDED SEAFOOD SALAD
(6-cup mold, lightly oiled)

1 envelope unflavored gelatin
¼ cup cold water
12 ounces tomato juice
6 ounces (2 3-ounce packages) cream cheese, diced
¾ cup mayonnaise
½ teaspoon Worcestershire sauce
2 tablespoons lemon juice
1½ cups shrimp, cooked and chopped
1½ cups crab meat, cooked and flaked
1 tablespoon grated onion
¼ cup finely chopped celery
¼ cup finely chopped green bell pepper
Salad greens (for garnish)

Soften the gelatin in the cold water. Heat the tomato juice
and gradually add the cream cheese. Beat until smooth. Add
the softened gelatin, stirring until gelatin is dissolved. Remove from heat. Add the mayonnaise, Worcestershire, and
lemon juice, mixing well. Chill until slightly thickened, stirring occasionally.
   Combine the shrimp, crab meat, onion, celery, and green

pepper. Fold into the thickened gelatin. Turn into the prepared mold and chill until set.

Unmold, using Method 3. Garnish with salad greens.

SMOKED TROUT MOUSSE
(4-cup mold, lightly oiled)

1 medium smoked trout
¼ cup milk
¾ cup water
1 envelope unflavored gelatin
¼ cup dry white wine
1 tablespoon butter
2 tablespoons finely chopped onion
1 tablespoon flour
1 cup milk
¾ cup mayonnaise
2 hard-cooked eggs
Salt and pepper to taste
½ cup heavy cream, whipped

Gently poach the trout in the combined milk and water for about 8 to 10 minutes, or until fish easily flakes away from bones. Let stand in liquid until cool. Carefully lift the meat off the bones and flake.

Soften the gelatin in the white wine.

In a small saucepan, over low heat, melt the butter. Add the onion and cook until onion is transparent. Add the flour. Gradually add the milk, stirring constantly until mixture begins to thicken. Remove from heat. Add the softened gelatin, stirring until gelatin is dissolved.

Place the mayonnaise in a large mixing bowl. Separate the yolks from the hard-cooked eggs and force them through a sieve. Add to the mayonnaise. Chop the egg whites and add.

Stir in the warm sauce. Add salt and pepper to taste. Chill until slightly thickened.

Add the flaked trout. Fold in the whipped cream. Turn into the prepared mold and chill until set.

Unmold, using Method 3.

MOLDED TUNA SALAD
(4-cup mold, lightly oiled)

> 1 envelope unflavored gelatin
> $\frac{1}{4}$ cup cold water
> 1 can (10$\frac{1}{2}$ ounces) chicken broth, heated to boiling
> 1 teaspoon lemon juice
> $\frac{1}{2}$ cup mayonnaise
> 1 tablespoon grated onion
> 1 stalk of celery, grated or finely minced
> 1 tablespoon minced parsley
> 1 can (7 ounces) tuna, drained

Sprinkle gelatin over cold water and let soften for about 5 minutes. Add to the hot chicken broth and stir until gelatin is dissolved. Cool slightly.

Add the lemon juice and mayonnaise. Chill until slightly thickened.

Add the onion, celery, parsley, and tuna. Turn into the prepared mold and chill until set.

Unmold, using Method 3.

VEGETABLE MOLDS

Surrounded by crisp, green leafy garnish, vegetable molds make a delightful first course or side dish. As such, individual molds are very attractive.

Jelled in ring form, vegetable molds are perfect for filling with your favorite meat or seafood salad. Such a mold can be a most eye-appealing and delicious main course. The entire dish offers a pleasing contrast in food textures between the cold smoothness of the gelatin and the crunchy roughness of the salad filling.

On a hot summer day or evening when appetites are small, the vegetable recipes in this chapter can be very tempting indeed.

ARTICHOKE HEARTS IN WINE ASPIC
(6-cup mold, dipped in cold water)

3¼ cups cold chicken stock, fat removed from surface
2 eggshells, wiped clean and crushed
2 egg whites, beaten until frothy
2 envelopes unflavored gelatin
⅔ cup dry white wine
4 raw mushrooms, wiped clean and sliced
2 packages (9 ounces each) frozen artichoke hearts,* cooked
　　as directed, drained and chilled

Place the cold chicken stock in a large stainless-steel or enamel pan of about 3-quart capacity. Slowly heat until the stock is melted and slightly warm. Add the eggshells and egg whites. Continue cooking over medium heat, folding in the egg whites so that they come in contact with the stock at the bottom of the pan. Stop stirring when the mixture begins to boil. Let mixture rise to the top of the pan, then quickly turn off the heat and remove pan from the burner. Let the mixture settle and gently push the coagulated egg whites to one side so that you can see how clear the stock is. If it is still cloudy, return mixture to a boil again (without stirring), let it rise to the top of the pan and remove from the heat.

Rinse a clean dish towel or other piece of heavy cloth in cold water and wring out. Line a large strainer with the cloth and place over a bowl. Carefully strain the clarified stock into the bowl. Do *not* wring out the cloth into the stock.

Soften the gelatin in the white wine for 5 minutes. Add it to the hot clarified stock, stirring until gelatin is dissolved. Pour a thin layer of the gelatin stock into the bottom of the mold and chill until set.

Using the sliced raw mushrooms, arrange a design in the

* Other cooked vegetables may be substituted for the artichoke hearts, if desired.

mold on top of the set aspic. Carefully ladle a little more syrupy aspic over the mushrooms to set the pattern. Chill until set.

Using the cooked and chilled artichoke hearts, arrange a few in the mold on top of the set mushroom design. Spoon in another layer of aspic to cover; chill.

Continue alternating the artichoke hearts and aspic until all is used up and the mold is full. Chill until completely set.

Unmold, using Method 1 or 2.

ASPARAGUS MOUSSE I
(4-cup ring mold, lightly oiled)

1 envelope unflavored gelatin
1/4 cup cold water
1 can (14 1/2 ounces) asparagus spears, drained (reserve liquid)
1/2 cup mayonnaise
1 teaspoon onion juice
1 teaspoon Worcestershire sauce
Salt and pepper to taste
1 cup heavy cream, whipped

Sprinkle gelatin over water in a heat-resistant cup and let stand for 5 minutes to soften. Place cup in a pan of hot water over low heat, stirring until gelatin is dissolved.

In a blender, purée the asparagus spears, mayonnaise, onion juice, and Worcestershire sauce; add salt and pepper to taste. Combine the purée, dissolved gelatin, and asparagus liquid, mixing well. Chill until slightly thickened, stirring occasionally.

Fold in the whipped cream. Turn into the prepared mold and chill until set.

Unmold, using Method 3.

ASPARAGUS MOUSSE II
(8-cup mold, lightly oiled)

1½ envelopes unflavored gelatin
2 cups consommé
2 tablespoons brandy or sherry
2 cans (14½ ounces each) asparagus spears, drained
6 stuffed olives, sliced
¾ cup mayonnaise
1 teaspoon onion juice
2 teaspoons Worcestershire sauce
Salt and pepper to taste
1 cup heavy cream, whipped

Make an aspic: Sprinkle the gelatin over the consommé in a small saucepan and dissolve over low heat. When cooled, stir in the brandy. Cover the bottom of the prepared mold with a thin layer of aspic and chill until very thick.

Arrange a few of the asparagus spears and the sliced olives in a design in the mold on the chilled aspic. Pour another layer of aspic to set the pattern and chill until very thick. Set aside the remaining aspic, but do not chill.

In a blender, purée the remaining asparagus with the mayonnaise, onion juice, and Worcestershire sauce. Add the purée to the remaining aspic and mix well. Add salt and pepper to taste. Chill until slightly thickened, stirring occasionally.

Fold in the whipped cream. Turn into the chilled mold and refrigerate until set.

Unmold, using Method 1 or 2.

AVOCADO MOUSSE I
(4-cup ring mold, lightly oiled)

1 package (3 ounces) lime-flavored gelatin
1 cup boiling water
2 ripe avocados, peeled and pitted
½ cup mayonnaise
1 tablespoon lemon or lime juice
⅛ teaspoon salt
1 cup heavy cream, whipped

Dissolve the gelatin in the boiling water. Set aside to cool.

Purée the avocados, mayonnaise, and juice in a blender. Combine the gelatin mixture with the avocado purée and add the salt. Chill until slightly thickened, stirring occasionally.

Fold in the whipped cream. Turn into the prepared mold. Chill until set.

Unmold, using Method 3.

AVOCADO MOUSSE II
(5-cup ring mold, lightly oiled)

1½ envelopes unflavored gelatin
3 cups flavored consommé
2 tablespoons brandy
3 ripe avocados
Lemon juice
5 raw mushrooms, sliced
1 teaspoon grated onion
1 teaspoon Worcestershire sauce
½ cup mayonnaise
Salt and pepper to taste
½ cup heavy cream, whipped

Make an aspic: Sprinkle the gelatin over the consommé in a small saucepan and dissolve over low heat. When cooled, stir in the brandy. Cover the bottom of a ring mold with a thin layer of the aspic and chill until very thick. Set aside the remaining aspic, but do not chill.

Cut the avocados in half (the long way) and remove the pits. Peel the avocado halves and cut into thin slices, forming crescents. Sprinkle with lemon juice. On top of the chilled aspic in the mold, arrange a design using the mushrooms and some avocado crescents. Carefully pour another layer of liquid aspic over them to set the pattern and chill until very thick.

In a blender, purée the remaining avocado slices with the grated onion, Worcestershire, and mayonnaise. Combine with the remaining liquid aspic and add salt and pepper to taste. Chill until slightly thickened, stirring occasionally.

Fold in the whipped cream. Turn into the chilled mold and refrigerate until set.

Unmold, using Method 1 or 2.

THREE-BEAN SALAD MOLD
(4-cup mold, dipped in cold water)

1 envelope unflavored gelatin
1¾ cups tomato or V-8 (or similar) juice, divided
1 teaspoon sugar
1 tablespoon lemon juice
Salt and pepper to taste
1 package (10 ounces) frozen baby lima beans
1 can (8 ounces) red kidney beans, drained
1 can (8 ounces) garbanzo beans, drained
2 tablespoons finely chopped parsley
¼ cup chopped scallions
2 tablespoons vinegar
1 clove garlic, crushed

In a small heat-resistant cup, sprinkle gelatin over ¼ cup of tomato juice and let stand 5 minutes to soften. Place cup in a pan of hot water over low heat, gently stirring until gelatin is dissolved. Add sugar to the hot gelatin and stir until sugar is dissolved. Pour gelatin mixture into the remaining 1½ cups tomato juice. Add the lemon juice and salt and pepper to taste. Chill until slightly thickened, stirring occasionally.

Prepare lima beans as label directs; drain. In a mixing bowl, combine the three types of beans with the parsley, scallions, vinegar, and garlic. Cover and chill until the tomato base is ready for use.

Fold the marinated beans into the gelatin mixture. Turn into the prepared mold and chill until set.

Unmold, using Method 1 or 2.

BEET BORSCHT SALAD MOLD
(6-cup mold, lightly oiled)

2 envelopes plus 1½ teaspoons unflavored gelatin
½ cup cold water
1 (1 pound) can or jar sliced beets, drained (reserve liquid)
12-ounce can tomato juice
¼ cup lemon juice
1 can (10½ ounces) beef consommé
1¼ teaspoons salt
⅛ teaspoon pepper
1 teaspoon sugar
1 cup sour cream
Watercress (for garnish)

Sprinkle gelatin over water in a heat-resistant cup and let stand for 5 minutes to soften. Place cup in a pan of hot water over low heat, stirring until gelatin is dissolved. Set aside to cool.

Reserve about 6 slices of beet for decoration. Mash the rest of the beets through a sieve or in a blender. Combine beet liquid, tomato juice, lemon juice, consommé, salt, pepper, and sugar. Add dissolved gelatin and mix well. Chill until slightly thickened.

Whisk in sour cream and mashed beets until mixture is smooth and evenly colored. Turn into the prepared mold and chill until set.

Unmold, using Method 3. Garnish with the beet slices, cut into fancy shapes, and watercress.

Serve with additional sour cream and pumpernickel bread.

BROCCOLI MOUSSE
(6-cup mold, lightly oiled)

1 envelope plus 2 teaspoons unflavored gelatin
$\frac{1}{2}$ cup cold milk
2 packages (10 ounces each) frozen chopped broccoli, thawed
$\frac{1}{4}$ cup chopped onion
2 cups chicken broth
2 teaspoons salt
$\frac{1}{8}$ teaspoon mace
$\frac{1}{4}$ teaspoon white pepper
1 cup heavy cream, whipped

Sprinkle the gelatin over the milk in a small heat-resistant cup. Let stand for 5 minutes to soften. Place cup in a pan of hot water over low heat, stirring until gelatin is dissolved.

In a medium-sized pan, combine broccoli, onion, and chicken broth. Bring to a boil and simmer for about 10 minutes, or until broccoli is tender. Add the salt, mace, and pepper. Pour into a blender and purée until smooth. Return purée to the pan and stir in the dissolved gelatin, mixing well. Chill until cool and slightly thickened, stirring occasionally.

Fold in the whipped cream. Turn into the prepared mold and chill until set.

Unmold, using Method 3.

CARROT MOUSSE
(4-cup ring mold, lightly oiled)

6 carrots, sliced
1 medium onion, sliced
1 stalk celery, sliced
1½ cups chicken broth
1 teaspoon salt
¼ teaspoon sugar
⅛ teaspoon cayenne pepper
1 envelope unflavored gelatin
½ cup cold water
¾ cup heavy cream, whipped

Boil the carrots, onion, celery, chicken broth, salt, and sugar about 15 minutes, or until vegetables are tender. Drain, reserving the liquid. Mash the vegetables through a sieve or in a blender. Add the cayenne pepper.

Sprinkle gelatin over water in a heat-resistant cup and let stand for 5 minutes to soften. Place cup in a pan of hot water over low heat, stirring until gelatin is dissolved. Add to the reserved cooking liquid. Blend in the carrot purée and the sour cream, mixing well. Chill until slightly thickened, stirring occasionally.

Fold in the whipped cream. Turn into the prepared mold and chill until set.

Unmold, using Method 3.

MINTED CARROT MOUSSE
(4-cup ring mold, lightly oiled)

6 carrots, sliced
1½ cups chicken broth
1 teaspoon salt
¼ teaspoon sugar
⅛ teaspoon cayenne pepper
¼ teaspoon paprika
1 tablespoon chopped fresh mint
1 envelope unflavored gelatin
½ cup cold water
¾ cup heavy cream, whipped

Boil the carrots, chicken broth, salt, and sugar for about 15 minutes or until carrots are tender. Drain, reserving the liquid. Mash the carrots through a sieve or in a blender. Add the cayenne pepper, paprika, and mint.

Sprinkle the gelatin over the water in a heat-resistant cup and let stand for 5 minutes to soften. Place cup in a pan of hot water over low heat, stirring until gelatin is dissolved. Add to the reserved liquid. Blend in the carrot purée, mixing well. Chill until slightly thickened, stirring occasionally.

Fold in the whipped cream. Turn into the prepared mold and chill until set.

Unmold, using Method 3.

SHREDDED CARROT GELATIN
(4-cup mold, dipped in cold water)

1 package (3 ounces) lemon-flavored gelatin
1 cup boiling water
2 tablespoons lemon juice or white wine vinegar
1 teaspoon salt
1 cup cold water
2 cups shredded carrots
1 teaspoon chopped chives
1 teaspoon chopped parsley

Dissolve the gelatin in the boiling water. Add the lemon juice, salt, and cold water and chill until slightly thickened, stirring occasionally.

Stir in the carrots, chives, and parsley. Turn into the prepared mold and chill until set.

Unmold, using Method 1 or 2.

CAULIFLOWER-TOMATO ASPIC
(6-cup mold, lightly oiled)

1 small head fresh cauliflower or 1 package, frozen
1 envelope unflavored gelatin
2/3 cup cold water
1 cup tomato juice
6 ounces cream cheese, softened
1 cup mayonnaise
1 tablespoon grated onion
1 stalk celery, grated
8 black olives, chopped

Steam the fresh cauliflower about 8 minutes, or until cooked but still firm. If using frozen cauliflower, cook according to package directions. Drain and cool. Break into flowerets.

Soften the gelatin in the cold water for 5 minutes. Heat the tomato juice and add the softened gelatin, stirring over low heat until gelatin is dissolved. Add the cream cheese, stirring until cheese is melted and well mixed. Remove from heat and cool slightly.

Add the mayonnaise and taste for seasoning. Chill until slightly thickened, stirring occasionally.

Fold in the onion, celery, olives, and flowerets. Turn into the prepared mold and chill until set.

Unmold, using Method 3.

MOLDED COLESLAW
(5-cup mold, lightly oiled)

> 1 envelope unflavored gelatin
> 1/4 cup cold water
> 1 cup boiling water
> 1 tablespoon sugar
> 3/4 teaspoon salt
> 2 tablespoons vinegar
> 3/4 cup mayonnaise
> 1 small onion, grated
> 1 1/2 cups finely shredded green cabbage
> 1 cup finely shredded carrots
> 1 teaspoon celery seed
> 1/3 cup white raisins (optional)

Soften the gelatin in the cold water for 5 minutes. Dissolve the gelatin in the boiling water. Add the sugar and salt and stir until they are dissolved. Add the vinegar. Cool slightly.

Stir in the mayonnaise and grated onion. Taste for seasoning. Cover and chill until slightly thickened.

Stir in the green cabbage, carrots, celery seed, and raisins. Mix well. Turn into the prepared mold and chill until set. Unmold, using Method 3.

CUCUMBERS IN YOGURT MOLD
(5-cup mold, dipped in cold water)

    4 cucumbers
    1 teaspoon salt
    1 tablespoon sugar
    1 tablespoon lemon juice
    Cold water
    1 envelope plus 1½ teaspoons unflavored gelatin
    3 containers (8 ounces each) plain yogurt
    ¼ cup chopped fresh mint

Peel the cucumbers and cut them in half lengthwise. Remove and discard the seeds. Chop the halves into small morsels, ¼- to ½-inch square. Sprinkle with the salt, sugar, and lemon juice. Toss lightly and place in the refrigerator for at least 1 hour.

Drain off the accumulated liquid into a measuring cup. Add cold water to this liquid to make 1 cup. Pour into a small saucepan. Sprinkle the gelatin over the liquid and let stand for 5 minutes to soften. Place over low heat, stirring until gelatin is dissolved. Chill until slightly thickened.

Add the yogurt and beat with a rotary beater or whisk until smooth. Add the mint and cucumber morsels, including any additional liquid they may have accumulated in the meantime. Taste for seasoning. Turn into the prepared mold and chill until set.

Unmold, using Method 3.

MINTED CUCUMBER MOUSSE
(4-cup mold, lightly oiled)

    1 package (3 ounces) lime-flavored gelatin
    1 cup boiling water
    ½ cup mayonnaise
    1 cup sour cream
    3 medium cucumbers, peeled, seeded, and grated
    1 tablespoon chopped chives
    1 tablespoon chopped mint leaves
    1 tablespoon grated lime rind
    ½ teaspoon salt

Dissolve the gelatin in the boiling water. Cool.

In a mixing bowl, combine the remaining ingredients, grating the cucumbers directly into the cream mixture so they do not discolor. Mix well. Add the dissolved gelatin, folding in until well blended. Turn into the prepared mold and chill until set.

Unmold, using Method 3.

GAZPACHO SALAD MOLD
(4-cup mold, lightly oiled)

    1 envelope unflavored gelatin
    12 ounces tomato juice
    ¼ cup lemon juice
    ¼ teaspoon hot pepper sauce
    1 clove garlic, crushed
    1 small onion, grated
    ½ teaspoon salt
    1 green pepper, finely chopped
    1 cucumber, peeled, seeded, and finely chopped
    1 large tomato, peeled and chopped

In a small saucepan, sprinkle the gelatin over the tomato juice and let stand for 5 minutes to soften. Place over low heat and stir constantly until gelatin is dissolved. Cool.

Combine the lemon juice, pepper sauce, garlic, onion, and salt in a mixing bowl. Add the tomato gelatin and mix well. Chill until slightly thickened, stirring occasionally.

Stir in the green pepper, cucumber, and tomato. Turn into the prepared mold and chill until set.

Unmold, using Method 1 or 2.

FRESH GREEN BEAN MOUSSE
(5- to 6-cup mold, lightly oiled)

1¼ pounds young, tender green beans, sliced
1 medium onion, sliced
1½ cups chicken broth
1 teaspoon salt
¼ teaspoon sugar
⅛ teaspoon white pepper
⅛ teaspoon nutmeg
1 envelope plus 1 teaspoon unflavored gelatin
¼ cup cold water
½ cup sour cream
½ cup heavy cream, whipped

Boil the green beans, onion, chicken broth, salt, sugar, and pepper for about 15 minutes, or until vegetables are tender. Drain, reserving the liquid. Purée about three-quarters of the vegetables in a blender or force through a food mill. Chop the remaining beans and add them to the purée. Add the nutmeg.

Sprinkle the gelatin over the water in a small heat-resistant cup and let stand for 5 minutes to soften. Place cup in a pan of hot water over low heat, gently stirring until gelatin is dissolved. Add to the reserved cooking liquid. Stir in the vegetable mixture and the sour cream, mixing well. Chill until slightly thickened, stirring occasionally.

Fold in the whipped cream. Turn into the prepared mold and chill until set.

Unmold, using Method 3.

MUSHROOMS IN ASPIC
(4 individual molds, dipped in cold water)

1 envelope unflavored gelatin
¼ cup cold water
1¾ cups chicken broth
1 small onion, peeled
1 bay leaf
6 peppercorns
2 tablespoons butter
½ pound fresh small button mushrooms, thinly sliced
1 tablespoon chopped fresh parsley
4 tablespoons cooked rice

Sprinkle the gelatin over the cold water to soften. In a saucepan, combine the chicken broth with the onion, bay leaf, and peppercorns. Bring to a boil and simmer gently for 20 minutes. Remove the onion, bay leaf, and peppercorns. Add the gelatin and stir until it is dissolved. Set aside to cool. Chill until slightly thickened.

Melt the butter in a medium fry pan. Add the mushrooms and cook quickly over medium-high heat until lightly browned. Stir into the thickened gelatin. Add the parsley and rice and mix well. Turn into the prepared molds and chill until set.

Unmold, using Method 4.

Serve on lettuce.

COTTAGE POTATO RING
(4-cup ring mold, lightly oiled)

> 1 envelope unflavored gelatin
> 1 cup cold milk
> 2 cups mashed potatoes
> ½ teaspoon dillweed
> 1 cup cottage cheese
> 2 tablespoons chopped chives
> Salt and pepper to taste

Sprinkle the gelatin over the cold milk in a heat-resistant cup and let stand for 5 minutes to soften. Place cup in a pan of hot (not boiling) water over low heat, stirring until gelatin is dissolved. Combine with the remaining ingredients, mixing well. Turn into the prepared mold and chill until set.

Unmold, using Method 3.

To serve, fill ring with your favorite meat or vegetable salad.

Variation

Sour Cream Potato Ring

Substitute 1 cup sour cream for the 1 cup cottage cheese.

MOLDED POTATO SALAD
(8-cup mold, lightly oiled)

1 envelope mild Italian salad dressing mix
4 tablespoons vinegar
4 cups peeled, diced cooked potatoes
3 strips bacon, crisply fried and crumbled
1 envelope unflavored gelatin
1 cup apple juice, divided
1 cup mayonnaise
1 cup sour cream
1 tablespoon grated onion
1 Delicious (red) apple, cored
Salt and pepper to taste

Combine the Italian salad dressing mix with the vinegar. Pour over the potatoes and bacon. Cover and marinate in the refrigerator for at least 1 hour.

In a small heat-resistant cup, sprinkle the gelatin over ¼ cup of apple juice and let stand 5 minutes to soften. Place cup in a pan of hot water over low heat, stirring until gelatin is dissolved. Add to the remaining ¾ cup of apple juice. Stir in the mayonnaise and sour cream. Chill until slightly thickened, stirring occasionally.

Add the onion. Chop the apple with skin directly into the chilled mixture. Add the marinated potatoes and bacon. Mix well. Taste for seasoning. Add salt and pepper, if necessary. Turn into the prepared mold and chill until set.

Unmold, using Method 3.

RED-AND-GREEN RICE SALAD MOLD
(4-cup mold, lightly oiled)

2 teaspoons unflavored gelatin
¼ cup cold water
½ cup mayonnaise
½ cup sour cream
2 tablespoons lemon juice
3 cups cold cooked rice
2 tablespoons chopped parsley
1 tablespoon chopped chives
½ teaspoon salt
¼ teaspoon white pepper
1 green bell pepper, finely chopped
1 sweet red pepper, finely chopped

In a small heat-resistant cup, sprinkle the gelatin over the water and let stand for 5 minutes to soften. Place cup in a pan of hot water over low heat, stirring until gelatin is dissolved.

In a large mixing bowl, combine the mayonnaise, sour cream, and lemon juice. Stir in the dissolved gelatin, mixing well. In another bowl, combine the rice with the remaining ingredients. Add to the mayonnaise-gelatin mixture. Turn into the prepared mold and chill until set.

Unmold, using Method 3.

MOLDED SPINACH SALAD
(5-cup mold, lightly oiled)

1 envelope unflavored gelatin
⅓ cup cold water
1 can (10½ ounces) beef consommé
¼ teaspoon salt
2 tablespoons lemon juice

1 small onion, grated
1 package (10 ounces) frozen chopped spinach, thawed and
    drained, or 1½ cups fresh raw spinach, chopped
2 hard-cooked eggs, peeled and chopped
½ pound bacon, cooked crisp and crumbled
¼ pound fresh mushrooms, thinly sliced

Sprinkle the gelatin over the cold water in a small heat-resistant cup and let stand for 5 minutes to soften. Place cup in a pan of hot water over low heat, stirring until gelatin is dissolved. Add to the beef consommé. Add the salt and lemon juice. Chill until slightly thickened.

Add the remaining ingredients, mixing well. Turn into the prepared mold and chill until set.

Unmold, using Method 1 or 2.

PECAN-SQUASH MOUSSE
(5-cup mold, lightly oiled)

1 cup seasoned chicken broth, cold
1 envelope plus 1 teaspoon unflavored gelatin
2 packages (12 ounces each) frozen cooked squash
4 tablespoons brown sugar
½ cup chopped pecans
1 cup heavy cream, whipped

Remove any fat from the surface of the cold chicken broth. Sprinkle the gelatin over the broth and let stand for 5 minutes to soften.

Prepare the frozen squash according to package directions. Stir in the brown sugar. Add the softened gelatin to the hot squash. Reheat and simmer the broth-squash mixture for 5 minutes, stirring until the gelatin is dissolved. Chill until slightly thickened.

Whisk the thickened mixture until smooth. Add the chopped pecans. Fold in the whipped cream. Turn into the prepared mold and chill until set.

Unmold, using Method 3.

TOMATO ASPIC RING
(4-cup ring mold, dipped in cold water)

    2 envelopes unflavored gelatin
    ½ cup cold water
    3 cups tomato juice, divided
    1 tablespoon grated onion
    1 envelope Italian salad dressing mix
    1 tablespoon lemon juice
    ½ teaspoon sugar
    Salt and pepper to taste

Soften the gelatin in the water for 5 minutes.

In a saucepan, combine 1 cup of tomato juice with the onion, Italian dressing mix, lemon juice, and sugar. Bring to a boil and simmer for 5 minutes. Remove from heat. Stir in the softened gelatin until dissolved. Add to the remaining 2 cups of tomato juice. Mix well and add salt and pepper to taste. Turn into the prepared mold and chill until set.

Unmold, using Method 1 or 2.

To serve, fill the ring with salad greens lightly tossed with your favorite dressing.

WATERCRESS VICHYSSOISE MOLD
(6-cup mold, lightly oiled)

1 leek (white part), sliced
1 small onion, peeled and sliced
3 medium potatoes, peeled and sliced
2 cups chicken broth
½ teaspoon salt*
⅛ teaspoon white pepper
½ teaspoon chopped chives
½ cup minced watercress
2 envelopes unflavored gelatin
1 cup cold milk
1 cup heavy cream, whipped

In a medium saucepan, combine the leek, onion, potatoes and chicken broth. Bring to a boil, cover and let simmer for 30 minutes. Purée in a blender or mash and beat with a mixer until smooth. Add the salt and pepper; cool slightly. Add the chives and watercress.

In a heat-resistant cup, sprinkle the gelatin over the cold milk and let stand for 5 minutes to soften. Place cup in a pan of hot water, over low heat, gently stirring until gelatin is dissolved. Mix into the potato mixture. Chill until cool and slightly thickened, stirring occasionally.

Fold in the whipped cream. Turn into the prepared mold and chill until set.

Unmold, using Method 3.

* If chicken broth is pre-seasoned, less salt may be used.

FRUIT SALADS

Delicious molded fruit salads are the most versatile of dishes. They can be used as appetizers, light luncheon dishes, a side dish with the main course, and desserts. Begin with the recipes in this chapter and go on to create your own combinations. Make them often and serve them a different way each time. They are especially good in the hot summer months.

MOLDED APPLE SALAD
(3-cup mold, dipped in cold water)

   1 envelope unflavored gelatin
   ¼ cup cold water
   1¾ cups apple juice
   2 Delicious (red) apples, cored and sliced*
   1 teaspoon grated orange rind

* To prevent apples from turning brown after being sliced, cover them with cold water and add 2 tablespoons of lemon juice. They will keep white until ready for use.

Sprinkle the gelatin over the cold water in a small heat-resistant cup and let stand for 5 minutes to soften. Place cup in a pan of hot water over low heat, stirring until gelatin is dissolved. Add to the apple juice. Pour a thin layer of juice mixture into the prepared mold and chill until set.

Arrange a few of the apple slices in a design on top of the set gelatin. Pour another thin layer of juice mixture over the pattern and chill until set. Chill the remaining juice mixture until thickened but not set.

Add the apples and orange rind to the slightly thickened gel. Turn into the mold on top of the set pattern and chill until set.

Unmold, using Method 1 or 2.

MOLDED APRICOT SURPRISE
(6-cup mold, dipped in cold water)

2 cans (17 ounces each) whole peeled apricots
1 envelope unflavored gelatin
1 package (3 ounces) peach- or apricot-flavored gelatin
1 cup boiling water
1 cup cold water
Walnut halves
4 ounces whipped cream cheese
½ cup chopped walnuts
6 dates, pitted and finely chopped

Drain the apricots, reserving the liquid. Remove pits. Measure the reserved liquid and add water to equal 1¾ cups in all (liquid and water combined). Measure out ¼ cup of this liquid into a small heat-resistant cup. Sprinkle the unflavored gelatin over the liquid in the cup to soften for 5 minutes.

Dissolve the peach gelatin in the boiling water. Add the

softened unflavored gelatin and stir until gelatin is dissolved. Reheat, if necessary. Both gelatins should be completely dissolved. Add the cold water and the remaining 1½ cups apricot liquid. Pour a thin layer into the bottom of the mold and chill until set. Chill the remaining gelatin until slightly thickened.

Remove the mold from the refrigerator when the thin layer has set. Arrange a design in the mold on the set gelatin with the walnut halves. Ladle another layer of gelatin over the walnuts and chill to set the pattern.

In a small mixing bowl, combine the cream cheese, chopped walnuts, and dates thoroughly. Fill the cavity of each apricot with a small spoonful of the cheese mixture. Press the apricot halves together so that the fruit retains its whole appearance.

When the walnut pattern has set in the mold, use about half the stuffed apricots to arrange another design. Place them in such a way that it will be easy to slice the mold without cutting the apricots. Cover with another layer of thickened gelatin and chill until set. After the first layer has set, repeat this step with the remaining apricots and thickened gelatin. Chill the finished mold completely.

Unmold, using Method 1 or 2.

Serve on lettuce leaves.

AVOCADO-PINEAPPLE SALAD
(4-cup mold, lightly oiled)

   1 package (3 ounces) lime-flavored gelatin
   1 cup boiling water
   ⅛ teaspoon salt
   1 can (8¼ ounces) crushed pineapple*

* Do not use fresh or frozen pineapple in this recipe as both contain an enzyme that resists the jelling process.

2 ripe avocados, peeled and pitted
½ cup mayonnaise
1 tablespoon lemon juice
½ cup heavy cream, whipped

Dissolve the gelatin in the boiling water. Add the salt and stir until salt is dissolved. Set aside to cool.

Drain the liquid from the pineapple. Purée the avocados, mayonnaise, pineapple juice, and lemon juice in a blender. Add the purée to the gelatin mixture. Chill until slightly thickened, stirring occasionally.

Beat the chilled purée with a rotary beater until smooth. Add the crushed pineapple, mixing well. Fold in the whipped cream. Turn into the prepared mold and chill until set.

Unmold, using Method 3.

BANANA-NUT MOUSSE
(4-cup mold, lightly oiled)

1 envelope unflavored gelatin
¼ cup cold water
1¼ cups cold milk
4 ripe bananas, peeled and mashed
¼ cup chopped walnuts
1 cup sour cream
Walnut halves (for garnish)

Sprinkle the gelatin over the water in a small heat-resistant cup and let stand for 5 minutes to soften. Place cup in a pan of hot water over low heat, stirring until gelatin is dissolved.

In a mixing bowl, combine the cold milk and the bananas.

Beat with a rotary beater until smooth. Add the dissolved gelatin. Stir in the walnuts and the sour cream. Mix thoroughly. Turn into the prepared mold and chill until set.

Unmold, using Method 3. Garnish with walnut halves.

BING CHERRY SALAD
(4-cup mold, dipped in cold water)

   1 package (3 ounces) cherry-flavored gelatin
   1 cup boiling water
   ½ cup port wine
   ½ cup orange juice
   1 pound fresh Bing cherries, pitted and halved

Dissolve the gelatin in the boiling water. Add the port wine and orange juice. Chill until slightly thickened.

Fold in the Bing cherries. Turn into the prepared mold and chill until set.

Unmold, using Method 1 or 2.

Serve on lettuce greens.

FRESH CITRUS SALAD RING
(6-cup ring mold, dipped in cold water)

   6 juice oranges
   3 large navel oranges
   4 large grapefruit
   12 juicy tangerines
   3 envelopes unflavored gelatin
   Sugar to taste
   ⅛ teaspoon salt

1 tablespoon each grated orange, grapefruit, and tangerine
rind
Shredded coconut (for garnish; optional)

Into three separate bowls, squeeze enough juice from each of
the three kinds of fruit to yield 2 cups each. Measure ½ cup
of each juice and pour each ½ cup into separate heat-resistant
cups. Sprinkle 1 envelope of gelatin into each cup containing ½ cup juice and let stand for 5 minutes to soften. Place
each cup in a pan of hot (not boiling) water, stirring until
the gelatin is dissolved. Return the dissolved gelatin-juice
mixture back to the larger bowl from which each juice came.
Add sugar to taste to each bowl (the grapefruit will require
more). Add ⅛ teaspoon salt to the grapefruit juice. Stir each
until the sugar is dissolved. Add the grated rind (orange to
orange, etc.). For layering, pour the orange gelatin into the
prepared mold first and chill until very thick. Leave the
grapefruit and tangerine gelatins at room temperature for the
time being.

When the orange gelatin is fairly well set, add the grapefruit layer and chill.

When the grapefruit layer is fairly well set, add the tangerine layer and chill until completely set.

Unmold, using Method 1 or 2.

Peel the remaining fruit and cut out the sections from
each, removing all skin and seeds, if any. Toss together in a
mixing bowl and sprinkle with sugar. Chill.

Once the gelatin is unmolded, fill the ring with the fresh
fruit sections.

Garnish the finished dish with shredded coconut, if desired.

CRANBERRY FRUIT SALAD
(4-cup mold, dipped in cold water)

1 envelope unflavored gelatin
½ cup orange juice
2 cups fresh cranberries
1¼ cups water
1 cup sugar
½ cup chopped nuts
¾ cup chopped celery

Soften the gelatin in the orange juice. In a saucepan, combine the cranberries, water, and sugar. Bring to a boil, stirring occasionally, and let simmer for about 5 minutes, or until the berries pop. Remove from heat. Add the softened gelatin and stir until gelatin is dissolved. Chill until slightly thickened.

Add the nuts and the celery. Turn into the prepared mold. Chill until set.

Unmold, using Method 1 or 2.

FRUIT NECTAR SALAD
(6-cup mold, dipped in cold water)

2 packages (3 ounces each) lemon-flavored gelatin
¾ cup boiling water
1 can (12 ounces) apricot nectar
1 can (17 ounces) crushed pineapple
1 can (17 ounces) diced peaches
1 cup seedless green grapes

Dissolve the gelatin in the boiling water. Add the apricot nectar. Drain the syrup from the pineapple and the peaches and combine the syrups. Pour 1 cup of the syrup into the gelatin mixture and discard the rest. (Add water if there is not enough syrup to equal 1 cup.) Chill the gelatin mixture until slightly thickened, stirring occasionally.

Combine the pineapple, peaches, and grapes. Fold into the thickened gelatin. Turn into the prepared mold and chill until set.

Unmold, using Method 1 or 2.

GRAPEFRUIT-AVOCADO MOLD
(4-cup mold, melon-shaped, if possible, dipped in cold water)

1 package (3 ounces) lemon-flavored gelatin
1 cup boiling water
1 large grapefruit, pink preferred
½ medium avocado, peeled, sliced, and brushed with lemon juice

Dissolve gelatin in boiling water. Peel the grapefruit, then section it over a bowl to catch the juice. Add enough water to juice to make ¾ cup and stir into the dissolved gelatin. Pour about 1 inch of the gelatin mixture into the bottom of the prepared mold and chill until thickened, but not set.

Arrange about half the grapefruit sections and half the avocado slices in alternate rows in the bottom of the mold. Spoon an additional small amount of the gelatin mixture over the fruit and chill to set the pattern.

Chill the remaining gelatin until slightly thickened. Gently pour it into the mold on top of the design. Arrange the remaining grapefruit and avocado slices where necessary. Chill until set.

Unmold, using Method 1 or 2. Garnish with additional grapefruit sections, if desired.

GRAPEFRUIT MIST
(4-cup mold, lightly oiled)

1 envelope unflavored gelatin
1½ cups grapefruit juice, cold, divided
½ cup sugar
⅛ teaspoon salt
¼ teaspoon vanilla extract
2 unbeaten egg whites
1 grapefruit, separated into sections (for garnish)

In a small saucepan, sprinkle the gelatin over ½ cup of grapefruit juice and let stand for 5 minutes to soften. Place over low heat, stirring until gelatin is dissolved. Add the sugar and salt to the hot liquid and mix well. Cool slightly.

Add mixture to the remaining 1 cup grapefruit juice. Add the vanilla. Chill until slightly thickened.

Add the unbeaten egg whites to the slightly thickened gelatin mixture. Beat on high speed until the mixture is fluffy and holds its shape, about 10 minutes. Turn into the prepared mold and chill until set.

Unmold, using Method 1 or 2. Garnish with grapefruit sections.

GREEN GRAPE-LIME MOUSSE WITH FRESH FRUITS
(Tall 5- to 6-cup mold, with sides lightly oiled)

2 packages (3 ounces each) lime-flavored gelatin
1 cup boiling water
2 cups cold water
1 cup seeded halved green grapes
1 cup sour cream
¼ cup chopped walnuts

Stir gelatin in boiling water until dissolved; then stir in cold water. Pour about ¼ cup of gelatin mixture into the pre- pared mold and chill until firm, but not set.

Arrange several of the grape halves (cut side up) on the thickened gelatin layer in the mold. Spoon an additional 2 or 3 tablespoons of the remaining gelatin over the grapes (it is not necessary to cover the grapes completely). Refrigerate until firm, but not set. (See Tips on Layering, pages 15–16.)

Fold the sour cream into the remaining gelatin mixture and chill until slightly thickened. Fold in remaining grapes and the nuts. Gently turn into the mold, over the nearly set lime-grape design and chill until set.

Unmold, using Method 1 or 2. Surround the mousse with fresh sliced fruits in season (apples, pears and bananas should be brushed with lemon juice to prevent darkening). If platter is not to be served immediately, cover lightly and refrigerate.

FROSTY GREEN-GRAPE SALAD
(8-cup mold, dipped in cold water)

1 envelope plus 1½ teaspoons unflavored gelatin
3 cups white grape juice, chilled, divided
⅓ cup sugar
2½ pounds seedless white grapes
3 unbeaten egg whites

In a small saucepan, sprinkle the gelatin over 1 cup of grape juice and let stand for 5 minutes to soften. Add the sugar and place over low heat, stirring until gelatin is dissolved. In a large mixing bowl, add the dissolved gelatin to the remaining 2 cups grape juice and mix well. Ladle a very thin layer into the bottom of the prepared mold and chill until very thick. Place the remaining grape gelatin mixture in the refrigerator to begin its chilling process.

When the gelatin in the mold is very thick, remove mold from the refrigerator. Choose several perfect grapes and arrange a design in the mold on top of the thin layer of set gelatin. Carefully ladle another thin layer of the still liquid gelatin over the grapes to set the pattern. Return the mold to the refrigerator and chill until very thick. Chill the remaining gelatin until slightly thickened but not completely set.

Remove the slightly thickened gelatin in the mixing bowl from the refrigerator. Add the unbeaten egg whites. Beat on high speed for about 10 minutes, or until the mixture is fluffy and holds its shape. Fold in the remaining grapes, reserving several small clusters for garnish. Carefully pour the mixture into the prepared mold, making sure not to upset the arranged pattern. Chill until set.

Unmold, using Method 1 or 2. Garnish with frosted grape clusters and grape leaves, if available.

To Frost Grape Clusters

    Small grape clusters
    1 egg white, beaten until foamy
    ½ to 1 cup sugar

Dip the clusters into the egg white, laying them on waxed paper as you work. Gently coat them with the sugar. Dry them on a cake rack for ½ hour. Repeat the dipping and coating process; dry thoroughly.

MELON-BALL SALAD
(4-cup mold, dipped in cold water)

    1 envelope unflavored gelatin
    ½ cup cold water
    ⅓ cup sugar

⅛ teaspoon salt
⅔ cup boiling water
½ cup orange juice
⅓ cup lemon juice
2 cups small melon balls

Soften the gelatin in the cold water for 5 minutes. Add the sugar and salt to the boiling water, stirring until they are dissolved. Remove from heat. Add the softened gelatin and stir until gelatin is dissolved. Cool slightly.

Add the orange juice and lemon juice. Chill until slightly thickened, stirring occasionally.

Pour a thin layer of the thickened gelatin into the prepared mold. On top of this layer, arrange a few of the choicest melon balls in a design. Spoon a bit more of the thickened gelatin over these balls and chill to set the pattern.

Combine the remaining melon balls with the remaining gelatin. Turn into the mold with the set pattern and chill until set.

Unmold, using Method 1 or 2.

ORANGE-PINEAPPLE GELATIN
(5-cup mold, dipped in cold water)

2 envelopes unflavored gelatin
2 cups pineapple juice, divided
1 cup orange juice
⅔ cup white wine
1 tablespoon lemon juice
1 can (8¼ ounces) pineapple chunks, drained*

Sprinkle the gelatin over ½ cup pineapple juice in a small heat-resistant cup and let stand for 5 minutes to soften. Place

* Do not use fresh or frozen pineapple in this recipe as both contain an enzyme that resists the jelling process.

cup in a pan of hot water over low heat, stirring until gelatin is dissolved.

In a mixing bowl, combine the remaining 1½ cups pineapple juice with the orange juice, white wine, and lemon juice. Add the dissolved gelatin and mix thoroughly. Chill until slightly thickened, stirring occasionally.

Stir in the pineapple chunks. Turn into the prepared mold and chill until set.

Unmold, using Method 1 or 2.

SPICED PEAR MOUSSE
(4-cup mold, lightly oiled)

    1 cup drained pear liquid, add water if necessary
    1 package (3 ounces) orange-flavored gelatin
    1 can (1 pound) pear halves, drained
    1 cup pear nectar, chilled
    1 tablespoon lemon juice
    ½ teaspoon ground allspice
    1 cup sour cream

Bring the 1 cup of pear liquid and water to boil in a small saucepan. Empty the package of orange-flavored gelatin into a mixing bowl. Pour the boiling liquid into the mixing bowl to dissolve the gelatin. (Note: Put a metal spoon in the bowl when pouring the hot liquid so that heat does not crack the bowl.) Stir with the spoon until the gelatin is dissolved.

Reserve 3 pear halves for garnish and mash the rest. Add to the dissolved gelatin and beat with a rotary beater until smooth. Add the pear nectar, lemon juice, allspice, and sour cream. Mix thoroughly. Turn into the prepared mold and chill until set.

Unmold, using Method 3. Garnish with the reserved pear halves.

Serve on lettuce.

MOLDED PINEAPPLE CREAM
(4-cup mold, lightly oiled)

1 package (3 ounces) lemon-flavored gelatin
1 cup boiling water
1 teaspoon salt
1 tablespoon cider vinegar
1 tablespoon Worcestershire sauce
1 tablespoon grated onion
1 cup sour cream
¼ cup mayonnaise
2 cans (20 ounces each) crushed pineapple, drained well*

Dissolve the gelatin in the boiling water. Stir in the salt until it is dissolved. Chill until slightly thickened.

Beat the thickened gelatin with a rotary beater until smooth, about 1 minute. Add the vinegar, Worcestershire, onion, sour cream, and mayonnaise. Beat until well blended. Fold in the pineapple. Turn into the prepared mold and chill until set.

Unmold, using Method 3.

PINEAPPLE–COTTAGE CHEESE MOLD
(4-cup mold, lightly oiled)

1 envelope unflavored gelatin
1 cup cold milk, divided
1⅓ cups cottage cheese
2 tablespoons sugar
1 cup crushed pineapple, drained*
1 tablespoon grated orange rind

* Do not use fresh or frozen pineapple in this recipe as both contain an enzyme that resists the jelling process. Drain the pineapple well, pressing down on it in a strainer to remove excess liquid.

Sprinkle gelatin over ¼ cup cold milk in a small heat-resistant cup and let stand for 5 minutes to soften. Place cup in a pan of hot water over low heat, stirring until gelatin is dissolved. Add to the remaining ¾ cup milk. Add the cottage cheese and sugar, mixing well. Chill until slightly thickened.

Add the pineapple and orange rind. Turn into the prepared mold and chill until set.

Unmold, using Method 1 or 2.

WALDORF SALAD MOUSSE
(6-cup mold, lightly oiled)

1 envelope unflavored gelatin
1¼ cups apple juice, divided
½ cup mayonnaise
3 Delicious (red) apples, cored and diced with skin on*
¾ cup finely chopped celery
⅓ cup raisins
½ cup chopped walnuts
1 cup heavy cream, whipped

Sprinkle the gelatin over ¼ cup of apple juice in a small heat-resistant cup and let stand for 5 minutes to soften. Place cup in a pan of hot (not boiling) water over low heat, stirring until gelatin is dissolved. Add to the remaining 1 cup of apple juice. Stir in the mayonnaise. Chill until slightly thickened but not completely set.

Beat until smooth. Add the apples, celery, raisins, and walnuts. Fold in the whipped cream. Turn into the prepared mold and chill until set.

Unmold, using Method 3.

* To prevent apples from turning brown after being diced, cover them with cold water and add 2 tablespoons of lemon juice. They will keep white until ready for use.

DECORATING MOLDED SALADS AND SAVORIES

Special occasions often provide the incentive to spend more time creating a beautiful dish, especially if it can all be prepared in advance. Aside from placing various garnishes around or atop your gelatin, it is possible to use your own imagination to create elaborate decorations that completely encase the gelatin in a glossy finish. There are basically two ways to do this.

1. Decorating from Within the Mold—With this method, you should use only a clear or a speckled aspic because of their transparency. Recipes for such aspics are given in this chapter. You will need a mold that is 2 cups larger than called for in your basic recipe. Once you have determined the size of the mold, you must make the aspic recipe in a quantity large enough to completely fill the mold. (A mousse that requires a 6-cup mold + 2 cups decorating space = 8 cups aspic.) Since aspic is a clear jell, the mold need only be dipped in cold water to prepare it for use.

Fill the mold to the top with aspic and refrigerate. The aspic will firm from the outside of the mold toward the middle. When it has set firmly about 1 inch from the sides, use a large spoon to ladle out the loose aspic into a metal pan for reuse. If the sides of the molded aspic are too thick, dip the spoon in hot water and then use to remove the excess of set aspic. Keep dipping the spoon in the hot water as you carve away to the desired thickness ($\frac{1}{2}$ to $\frac{3}{4}$ inch). The center (bottom) of the molded aspic may also be removed with the hot spoon, if desired.

Once the mold is lined with aspic, you may wish to add more decoration before filling. Choose one or several of the basic ingredients in your recipe. The decorations may even be cut into fancy shapes. Using a pair of tweezers, dip the decorations in the syrupy aspic (that spooned out earlier into the metal pan), which will now be used as a glue. Place the mold, up to the rim, in a basin of ice water. With the tweezers, firmly place the decorations against the set aspic in the mold. Hold the decorations in place for a few seconds until they set. If the syrupy aspic is not sticky enough, place the metal pan in another bowl of ice water to hasten the chilling process as you work. Finish forming your design all around the mold and place it in the refrigerator to set.

If the mold you wish to line with aspic is very shallow, such as a fish shape, it is not necessary to go through the entire procedure of completely filling the mold and then spooning out the excess aspic. With this method, 2 cups of aspic should be sufficient. Simply place the mold in a basin filled with ice. Chill the aspic over ice water until it is the consistency of a very thick syrup. Then, using a small basting brush, quickly coat the inside of the mold. Chill until completely set and give a second coating. Proceed as you would above for adding additional decorations.

This method of decoration is especially suitable for gelatins made with cream or mayonnaise, and any of the recipes given in this book will serve the purpose very nicely indeed. The one exception to this is, of course, the dessert recipes. Obviously, no one would care to eat a dessert or sweet covered in a meat or fish aspic, however pretty it might look.

FILLING: Prepare your filling, if you have not already done so, and let it cool. A warm filling might disarrange your design. Carefully turn it into the decorated mold and chill until completely set. Unmold, using Method 1 or 2.

LEFTOVER ASPIC: The leftover syrupy aspic may be reheated over low heat until liquid and used to create additional decorations or garnish. Choose a shallow pie plate or baking pan and dip it in cold water. Pour in the liquid aspic to at least ¼ inch thick and chill until set. Using Method 1 or 2, unmold the aspic onto a wet piece of aluminum foil.

You may now cut designs with a wet cookie cutter, or other shapes (squares, triangles, etc.) with a wet knife. The aspic may also be chopped with a wet knife. Place these designs and shapes or heaps of chopped aspic around the turned-out gelatin as further garnish.

When presenting this decorated gelatin to your guests, you will feel not only like an accomplished gourmet cook but like a great artist as well.

2. Decorating a Turned-Out Gelatin from the Outside— This method is somewhat like frosting a cake, although, like decorating method 1, it is not suitable for desserts or sweet gelatins. There are basically two types of coating (frosting) sauces used for this purpose: chaud-froid and aspic.

Chaud-froid is a flavored white glaze gelatin that provides a base or solid background upon which the other decorations are placed. Chaud-froid is to the cook what a blank canvas is to the artist. This glaze may be tinted with a few drops of food coloring to achieve a pastel effect, if desired. Several variations of suitable chaud-froid recipes follow in this chapter.

Aspic is a flavored transparent gelatin coating used to keep the decorations from drying out or discoloring. It also serves the purpose of a glossy varnish and must *always* be used as a final coating over chaud-froid. Several variations of suitable aspic recipes follow in this chapter.

Both of the above coating sauces are thicker than the usual gelatin because they are used to hold foods in place.

Note: This method of decoration is also suitable for cooked cold roasts, ham and other meats, poultry, or fish as well as molded savory gelatins.

Two cups each of aspic and chaud-froid should be sufficient for covering a mold. Once the coating sauces are prepared, pour each into a metal pan. (Metal chills quickly and the sauces can be reheated if they become too thick.) Place the pan containing the chaud-froid in a bowl filled with ice and a little water. Stir occasionally, until the mixture begins to thicken. Remove the pan from the ice when the chaud-froid has reached the consistency of very thick syrup. Using a small, clean basting brush, coat the top and sides of the turned-out gelatin. The chaud-froid should set quickly if the gelatin has been kept cold in the refrigerator. Chill until well set. If necessary, add a second coat and chill. The surface of the gelatin should be completely covered. If the final surface is lumpy, dip a small spatula or knife in hot water and gently smooth it over the hardened sauce. Do not worry about dripping onto the plate that holds the gelatin. These drips can easily be removed later on.

While the chaud-froid background is setting in the refrigerator, start chilling the aspic over ice, just as you did the chaud-froid. Now is also the time to prepare your decorations (see below). Plan your design and, using a toothpick, mark the design on the set chaud-froid. Once placed, the decorations are difficult to remove without leaving a mark. Using a toothpick or tweezers, dip the decorations in the thickened syrupy aspic. Do not use the chaud-froid for dipping, because it is not transparent. Place the decorations on the chaud-froid in the places you have marked. When the design is complete, chill until set.

Note: Some decorations, such as very thin leaves or others that are very tiny, may be too awkward to dip in the aspic before placing on the chaud-froid. In this case, you may place them without dipping and gently dab them with a coat of aspic after the design is complete.

Brush a final layer of aspic over the entire decorated mold to give it a finished gloss. Chill until set. Remove with a spoon or a knife any drips and spillage that have accumulated on the serving dish. Then gently wipe the plate with a damp cloth.

LEFTOVER ASPIC AND CHAUD-FROID: Both may be chilled separately, as in decorating method 1, above, and later cut into shapes or chopped for additional garnish around the serving dish.

Decorations—Decorations should always be made from edible foods. Use such ingredients as hard-cooked eggs, vegetables, fruits, shrimp, canned truffles, and nuts. Try to select foods that are colorful. Many of these can be cut or carved into fancy shapes. You will find a very sharp paring knife, a vegetable peeler, and one or two sets of aspic/garnishing cutters* to be invaluable utensils for this purpose. All decora-

* Aspic/garnishing cutters resemble cookie cutters in miniature. They usually range ½ inch, ¾ inch, and 1 inch in diameter. They are available in

tions should be thoroughly dried on paper toweling before being dipped and placed on the chaud-froid background. In most cases, the drying process is easier if you dry whatever ingredients you are using before cutting out the desired shapes.

Most vegetables, such as carrots, turnips, radishes, squash, and so forth, can be used raw. These must all be sliced *paper-thin*. (Use your vegetable peeler.) Once you have several slices prepared, dry them on paper toweling. You may then cut them into a variety of shapes.

Red and green bell peppers, on the other hand, are difficult to work with unless they are first blanched in boiling water. If possible, remove their waxy skins. They may then be sliced thin with a vegetable peeler, dried, and cut into shapes.

With some fruits and vegetables, you should use only thin peelings. Among these are potatoes, tomatoes, cucumbers, apples, oranges, plums. The pulp in these items is either too juicy for use or discolors too quickly. Dry the peelings on paper toweling to remove all excess moisture before cutting into shapes.

Berries should be used only if they are tiny, such as currants or baby blueberries. Otherwise, your design will be out of proportion.

Juicy fruits, such as berries, cherries, and grapes, should be used only whole and uncut. Othewise, they will drip their juices all over your perfect chaud-froid base. Likewise, beets, because they bleed, should be avoided entirely.

---

most gourmet and food specialty shops. If you cannot find them, it is easy enough to make your own. Use the metal tops from some old lipsticks. Using a pair of pliers, reshape the open end into your own designs; squares, ovals, hearts, and so forth. Wash them well and then sterilize them in boiling water. They are then ready for use. For very tiny cutters, apply the same make-your-own technique to pencils or pens that have an eraser tip. Remove the eraser and then reshape the eraser container or use as a tiny circle shape. These tiny circles can produce decorations that resemble berries if placed along a green stem in your design. If the cutout designs should get stuck inside your home-made cutters, they can easily be removed with a straight pin or needle.

Processed foods, such as olives, pickles, and pimientos, need only be sliced thin or peeled and then dried before cutting into shapes.

Certain leaves, such as fresh mint or small sprigs of fresh herbs, such as dill, are pretty enough to use whole. These need only be washed and flattened. Place the wet leaves between sheets of paper toweling and press inside a heavy book for a few minutes. Once your design is planned, these leaves may then be placed directly atop the chaud-froid. They are too fragile to dip in the aspic.

Hollow greens, such as leeks, scallions, and green onions, require more preparation. They should first be slit open lengthwise, then dipped quickly *once* in and out of boiling water, followed by a cold rinse. Spread the pieces apart where they have been slit, to expose the cooked matter within. Using a blunt knife or spoon, carefully scrape away this soft mush. Flatten the pieces between sheets of paper toweling inside a heavy book before cutting them into shapes. These may also be placed on the chaud-froid without prior dipping.

After you have prepared your selection of foods for decorations, you will be ready to work your design. Lay it all out on a cutting board first. This will allow you to be freely creative and to experiment with shapes and positions without spoiling your chaud-froid base. Once your design is completed on the cutting board, transfer it to the chaud-froid background, where you have gently marked the positions with a toothpick. Give a final overall coating or two of aspic.

In the event you wish to utilize special items for decorations that are not edible, such as clam shells, nut shells, and so forth, it is better to place them on the plate or platter that holds your gelatin, rather than using them directly on the food.

Do-Ahead Medallion Decorations—Although you are willing to spend extra time in decorating foods for a special affair, you may still be too busy to do everything, even if you begin the day before the event. In this case, it is possible to plan and make your decorations several days in advance. Do-ahead medallions can be used to decorate a large assortment of cold foods—meats (roasts or hams), poultry, fish, or molded gelatins—that you would otherwise not have time to decorate.

The medallions are made separately in a plate and are not more than ¼ inch thick. They can be prepared as much as five days in advance, provided they are well covered with plastic wrap and stored in the refrigerator inside airtight plastic bags or containers.

A medallion consists of three layers:

Bottom layer: A chaud-froid base.

Middle layer: A design or decoration, created from paper-thin strips of edible foods, placed atop the chaud-froid base (See Decorations, page 129.)

Top layer: Several coatings of clear aspic to completely cover the chaud-froid and the design.

When ready for use, remove the prepared medallion from the refrigerator and unwrap. Loosen the edges of the medallion with a sharp knife. Then, using your fingers or a spatula, gently lift the medallion out of the plate. The medallion will have a rubbery texture and can easily be handled. Simply lay it in place and tuck lots of parsley sprigs underneath the edges of the medallion as a final touch.

If you have time and wish to be ultra-elaborate, the food on which you are going to place the medallion can also be completely coated with chaud-froid and/or covered with transparent aspic. The flavors of these coatings should correspond with those of the medallion. This is very effective with canned hams, roasts of a simple shape, and whole fish. Remember that the food should be cooked and cold before coating.

W<small>HAT</small> Y<small>OU</small> W<small>ILL</small> N<small>EED</small> <small>TO</small> M<small>AKE</small> <small>A</small> M<small>EDALLION</small>:

1. A dish or plate with a well in the center. The medallion will be made inside the well. Therefore, you cannot use a plate that is completely flat. Likewise, do not attempt to make the medallion in a pan, pie plate, or bowl, as the high sides will make it difficult to remove the medallion. Use a dinner plate for a large medallion and a dessert or bread-and-butter plate for a small medallion. The shape of the plate is not important. It can be round, square, or oval so long as it is the correct size.

2. One recipe of chaud-froid: Jellied White Sauce (page 142), Jellied Mayonnaise (page 141), or Jellied Lime Sauce (page 140). You will use only a very small amount of this in making one medallion. If you wish to make several medallions, one recipe provides plenty of chaud-froid, so do have fun and experiment if you wish. Whatever chaud-froid is left over can be used later on (as a coating for the food on which the medallion is going to be placed, or molded separately in a pan to provide cutout decorations or to be chopped for additional garnish).

3. One recipe of clear aspic: Quick Aspic (page 135), Quick Wine Aspic (page 135), Basic Aspic (page 136), or No-Stock Fish Aspic (page 137). Again, you will need only a small amount of this, but the leftover aspic can be saved for another use.

T<small>O</small> M<small>AKE</small> <small>A</small> M<small>EDALLION</small>:

1. *Generously* oil the plate.

2. Pour a layer of liquid chaud-froid into the well to about half the depth of the well. You need only enough to thoroughly cover the bottom of the plate (about ⅛ inch thick). Chill until set. Cover and store the remaining chaud-froid in the refrigerator for another use.

3. On a cutting board, lay out your design, using the foods

you have prepared for this purpose. (See Decorations, page 129.) Using tweezers, transfer the design to the chilled base of chaud-froid.

4. Using a clean pastry brush or a small spoon, carefully spread a layer of cool but liquid aspic over the design. Chill. It will be necessary to repeat this step several times. Do not attempt to completely cover the design with the first layer of liquid aspic as parts of the decorations may float.

5. Once the design is covered and set with aspic, add a final layer of liquid aspic to completely cover the medallion and fill the well. (Be careful not to go beyond the well onto the edge of the plate. This will give your medallion an awkward shape.) Chill. When set, wrap well and store as described above.

Note: The medallion will keep nicely for up to five days. However, the longer it is kept, the more rubbery and less palatable it will become. Try to prepare it as close to the date needed as possible.

Pastry-Bag Decorations—It is also possible to pipe decorations directly onto savory gelatin molds if you are handy with a cake-decorating tube. For fine yellow lines and/or dots, use the writing tip and fill the bag with a mixture of 2 or 3 hard-cooked egg yolks sieved through a strainer and bound with a little mayonnaise. Eight ounces of cream cheese blended with a little mayonnaise or sour cream (and a few drops of food coloring, if desired) can be used with the larger tips for making flowers, stars, leaves, and so forth. Plain mayonnaise (tinted, if desired) may also be piped through a decorating tube.

QUICK ASPIC
(Yield: 2 cups)

 1 envelope unflavored gelatin
 1/4 cup cold water
 1 can (13 ounces) jellied chicken or beef consommé
 2 tablespoons sherry

Soften the gelatin in the water for 5 minutes. Heat the consommé and add the softened gelatin, stirring until gelatin is dissolved. Remove from heat. Add the sherry and cool.

QUICK WINE ASPIC
(Yield: 3½ cups)

 2 envelopes unflavored gelatin
 1/3 cup cold water
 2/3 cup dry white wine
 2½ cups jellied chicken or beef consommé

Soften the gelatin in the water and wine for 5 minutes. Heat the consommé and add the softened gelatin, stirring until gelatin is dissolved. Remove from heat and cool.

BASIC ASPIC

(Yield: 4 cups. Do not make less than this amount. Any left over will keep in the refrigerator and can be heated for reuse.)

3½ cups cold homemade seasoned stock (beef, chicken, veal, pork, or fish)
2 envelopes unflavored gelatin
¼ cup cold water
2 tablespoons port wine
1 tablespoon cognac or brandy
2 eggshells, wiped clean and crushed
2 egg whites, beaten until frothy

The homemade stock must be very cold for two reasons: so that you can easily remove all traces of fat that coagulate at the top when chilled and so that you can judge the thickness of the stock. Homemade stocks jell naturally when made with bones. The recipe above is for a loosely jelled stock or one that is very liquid. If you find that your stock is very firm, cut the quantity of gelatin in half (to 1 envelope) and increase the quantity of stock to 4 cups.

Sprinkle the gelatin over the combined water, port, and cognac. Let it stand to soften while you clarify the stock. Do not worry if the gelatin absorbs all the liquid; this is normal.

You will need a large enamel or stainless-steel pan about 3-quart capacity. Do not use any other type of pan as other surfaces tend to make the aspic cloudy. Place the cold stock in the pan and slowly heat until melted and slightly warm. Add the eggshells and egg whites. Continue cooking over low heat, folding in the egg whites so that they come in contact with the stock at the bottom of the pan. Stop stirring when the mixture begins to boil. Let the mixture rise to the top of the pan, then quickly turn off the heat and remove pan from the burner. Let the mixture settle and gently push the coagulated egg whites aside so that you can see how clear the stock is. If it is still cloudy, return it to a boil a second time (without stirring), let it rise to the top of the pan, and remove from the heat.

Rinse a clean dish towel or other piece of heavy cloth in cold water and wring out. Line a large strainer with the cloth and place over a bowl. Carefully strain the clarified stock into the bowl. Do *not* wring out the cloth into the stock.

Add the softened gelatin to the hot stock and stir until gelatin is dissolved. Divide the stock into 2 equal portions. Set one aside for storage. The other can be used for coating and decorating. When you are ready, simply place the pan of stock in a bowl of ice water and stir until mixture begins to set. If it gets too firm, reheat it and chill once more. This may be done as often as necessary.

NO-STOCK FISH ASPIC
(Yield: 3 cups)

  2 cups clam juice
  1 cup water
  ¼ cup tomato juice
  1 medium onion, skinned and halved
  1 bay leaf
  6 sprigs fresh parsley
  2 eggshells, wiped clean and crushed
  2 egg whites, lightly beaten
  2 envelopes plus 1 teaspoon unflavored gelatin
  1 cup dry white wine, divided

Place the first 6 ingredients in a large stainless-steel or enamel pan of about 3-quart capacity. Bring to a boil and simmer for 30 minutes. Strain and cool slightly.

Clean the pan and refill it with the warm stock. Add the eggshells and egg whites. Cook over medium heat, folding in the egg whites so that they come in contact with the stock at the bottom of the pan. Stop stirring when the mixture begins to boil. Let the mixture rise to the top of the pan, then quickly turn off the heat and remove pan from the burner.

Rinse a clean dish towel or other piece of heavy cloth in cold water and wring out. Line a large strainer with the cloth and place over a clean pan. Carefully strain the clarified stock into the pan. Do *not* wring out the cloth into the stock.

Soften the gelatin in ½ cup of white wine for 5 minutes. Add it to the hot clarified stock, stirring until gelatin is dissolved. Return to a boil and cook down to 2½ cups. Remove from heat. Add remaining ½ cup of white wine.

MADEIRA BEEF ASPIC
(Yield: 4 cups)

Make as for Basic Aspic (page 136), but use the following substitutions:

¼ cup tomato juice instead of cold water
¼ cup Madeira instead of port wine and cognac
3½ cups cold homemade seasoned beef stock

Soften the gelatin in the tomato juice. Add it to the warm stock and egg whites before stock comes to a boil.

SPECKLED HERB ASPIC
(Yield: 2 cups)

2 cups liquid aspic (Quick Aspic, page 135, or Basic Aspic, page 136)
3 tablespoons of either chopped parsley, dill, mint, or chives

Stir the aspic over a bowl of ice water. When it begins to thicken, add the 3 tablespoons of chopped herb.

SPECKLED CAVIAR ASPIC
(Yield: 2 cups)

> 2 cups liquid fish aspic (Basic Aspic, page 136, or No-Stock Fish Aspic, page 137)
> 1 tablespoon fresh lemon juice, strained
> 3 tablespoons red or black lumpfish caviar, rinsed and drained*

Combine the aspic and the lemon juice. Place over a bowl of ice water and stir until the mixture begins to thicken. Gently stir in the caviar.

SPECKLED CITRUS ASPIC
(Yield: 2 cups)

> 2 cups liquid aspic (Quick Aspic, page 135, or Basic Aspic, page 136)
> 3 to 4 tablespoons finely grated fresh citrus rind: orange, lemon, lime, grapefruit, etc.

Stir the aspic over a bowl of ice water. When it begins to thicken, add the grated citrus rind.

---

* The caviar sold in jars in supermarkets comes in two types. Salmon caviar consists of large eggs, while lumpfish has very tiny eggs. Only the lumpfish caviar is suitable for this recipe.

CHAUD-FROID
JELLIED LIME SAUCE (FOR HAM OR CHICKEN)
(Yield: 2½ cups)

2 packages (3 ounces each) lime-flavored gelatin
¾ cup boiling water
4 teaspoons prepared horseradish, drained
1 teaspoon lime or lemon juice
2 cups sour cream

Dissolve the gelatin in the boiling water. Let cool.

Add the horseradish and lime juice. Whisk in the sour cream. Chill until mixture is the consistency of a very thick syrup.

Remove from refrigerator and place container in a bowl of ice water while working. Remember to give an occasional stir so that mixture does not get lumpy. If the mixture becomes too firm, dip its container in and out of a bowl of warm water several times to loosen it. Two coatings of this sauce should be sufficient as a background covering for decorating. Add a final coating of clear aspic for a glossy sheen and to prevent decorations from drying out.

Note: This sauce has a pale-green tint. Add a few drops of green food coloring if a stronger shade is desired.

Variations

Different flavors of gelatin (lemon, orange, peach, etc.) may be substituted for the lime for a slight change of flavor and color. However, still use lime or lemon juice in the recipe to cut the sweetness of the fruit gelatin.

CHAUD-FROID
JELLIED MAYONNAISE
(Yield: 2 cups)

1 envelope unflavored gelatin
1/4 cup cold water
2 tablespoons heavy cream, at room temperature
2 cups mayonnaise, at room temperature

Sprinkle the gelatin over the cold water in a small heat-resistant cup and let stand for 5 minutes to soften. Place cup in a pan of hot water over low heat, stirring until gelatin is dissolved. Combine the heavy cream and the mayonnaise. Add the dissolved gelatin, stirring until smooth.

Since mayonnaise is very thick, it may not be necessary to chill this sauce before spreading, unless you prefer to work with a firmer substance. Do not use ice, however, to chill it. A bowl of cold water is sufficient to thicken this sauce, since it reacts very quickly to temperature changes. Likewise, if the sauce gets too firm or lumpy, just dip its container in and out of a bowl of warm water several times to loosen it.

Use this sauce as a background covering for decorating and give it a final coating of aspic for a glossy sheen. This is also necessary to prevent any decorations added to it from drying out. Remember to chill each layer of coating before adding the next.

Variations

MUSTARD MAYONNAISE

Omit the heavy cream and add 2 tablespoons Dijon mustard and 2 tablespoons dry white wine.

Dill Mayonnaise

Omit the heavy cream and add 3 tablespoons fresh chopped dill or 1½ tablespoons dried dillweed and 2 tablespoons sherry.

Herbed Green Mayonnaise

In a blender mix the 2 cups mayonnaise with 2 tablespoons chopped parsley, 1 tablespoon snipped chives, 1 tablespoon dried tarragon, and 1 teaspoon dried dillweed. Turn into a bowl and stir in the dissolved gelatin and the heavy cream.

Seafood Mayonnaise

Omit the heavy cream; decrease the mayonnaise to 1¾ cups; add ½ cup ketchup, 1 tablespoon lemon juice, 2 tablespoons horseradish, drained, and 1 tablespoon sherry.

CHAUD-FROID
JELLIED WHITE SAUCE
(Yield: 2½ cups)

   1 envelope unflavored gelatin
   ½ cup sherry or Madeira
   1½ cups cold milk, divided
   1 small onion, peeled and halved
   1 stalk celery, diced
   3 sprigs parsley, chopped
   3 tablespoons butter
   3 tablespoons flour
   ½ teaspoon salt
   ¼ teaspoon sugar
   ¾ cup heavy cream or half-and-half

Soften the gelatin in the sherry. In a small saucepan, combine ¾ cup cold milk with the onion, celery, and parsley. Bring to a boil and remove from the heat. Let stand for a few minutes.

In another saucepan, melt the butter. Remove from the heat. Add the flour, salt, and sugar, stirring until smooth. Add the remaining ¾ cup cold milk and stir over low heat until the mixture begins to thicken. Strain the hot milk into this mixture. Stir until smooth. Add the softened gelatin, stirring until gelatin is dissolved. Remove from heat. Stir in the heavy cream.

Leave at room temperature until ready to decorate. Place container of sauce in a bowl of ice water, stirring until sauce is the consistency of a very thick syrup. Apply to a turned-out gelatin as a background. If sauce gets too firm, gently reheat and chill again to the correct consistency.

This sauce should be given a final coating of aspic.

Note: A few drops of food coloring may be added to the sauce to give it a pastel tint.

DECORATING DESSERTS

Garnishes of fruits, chocolate, nuts, or candies are all suitable for decorating desserts. The most beautiful effects, however, can be achieved with whipped cream piped into various designs or patterns. There are two ways of doing this.

Aerosol whipped cream, which can be bought at the dairy counter of your supermarket, is very practical. The nozzle of these cans is usually manufactured so that the cream comes out in a design. This is especially useful for border or edging work. Remember to chill the cream well and shake thoroughly before using. Always work with the can turned completely upside down. Any tilting of the can will cause the cream to spatter. I always do a few practice designs on a cookie sheet first.

Stabilized Frosting Cream (recipe follows) is homemade whipped cream that can be used in a cake-decorating tube.

This cream is light but can still produce much the same results as cake frosting, with sharp and clear designs. Any left-over Frosting Cream can be piped into designs (flowers, stars, rosettes, etc.) on a cookie sheet and then frozen. The designs can then be removed to a plastic bag and stored in a freezer for weeks. Simply place the frozen shapes on any dessert. They are easy to handle when frozen and take only a few minutes to thaw once in place.

Note: Do not attempt to use whipped cream that has not been stabilized in a cake-decorating tube. The warmth of your hand and the squeezing causes the untreated cream to separate in the bag, and also produces soft, mushy designs.

STABILIZED FROSTING CREAM
(Yield: 2 cups)

1 teaspoon unflavored gelatin
5 teaspoons brandy, rum, or any liqueur
1 cup cold heavy cream
¼ cup confectioners' sugar

Chill all utensils in the refrigerator (bowl, beaters, pastry bag, and decorating tips). Also chill the dessert that is to be decorated.

In a small heat-resistant cup, sprinkle the gelatin over the brandy and let stand for 5 minutes to soften. Place cup in a pan of hot water over low heat, stirring until gelatin is dissolved. Remove from heat and gently stir until the dissolved gelatin reaches room temperature.

Beat the cream in the chilled bowl while the gelatin is cooling. (Remember to give the gelatin an occasional stir so that it does not solidify at the bottom of the cup.) When the cream is beaten to a medium consistency, stop beating. Add all the sugar and gelatin at once. Resume beating until the cream stands in stiff peaks. (Do not overbeat.)

Wash your hands with cold water. Immediately place the cream in the chilled pastry bag and decorate your dessert. Do not chill the stabilized cream before use, but rather work as quickly as you can. The decorated dessert may then be placed in the refrigerator, where it will keep nicely for up to two days. If possible, place it in a covered container so that it does not absorb any other food odors.

RELISHES AND ACCOMPANIMENTS

When you're planning on receiving guests, you want your table to look its best. Many cooks prepare beautiful meals and go to a lot of trouble garnishing. But then out come the mustard jars and condiment bottles. This is one of the most common ways to destroy a lovely setting.

Everyone would like to give the impression of being a thoughtful host/hostess, and the recipes that follow are just the right clincher to show that you have, indeed, thought of everything.

CAPER MOUSSE
(2-cup mold, lightly oiled)

   1 envelope unflavored gelatin
   ⅓ cup cold water
   1 tablespoon lemon juice
   1 cup mayonnaise
   1 cup sour cream
   3 tablespoons capers, drained and minced
   2 tablespoons minced scallions
   Salt and white pepper to taste

In a small heat-resistant cup, sprinkle the gelatin over the combined water and lemon juice and let stand for 5 minutes to soften. Place cup in a pan of hot water over low heat, stirring until gelatin is dissolved. Combine with the mayonnaise, sour cream, capers, and scallions and whisk until smooth. Add salt and white pepper to taste. Turn into the prepared mold and chill until set.

   Unmold, using Method 3.

   Serve as an accompaniment to cold fish, veal, or chicken.

CHESTNUT-APPLE MOUSSE
(8-cup mold, lightly oiled)

   3 egg yolks
   ¼ teaspoon salt
   1½ cups cold milk
   1 envelope plus 2 teaspoons unflavored gelatin
   1 jar (10 ounces) marron pieces in syrup

Honey
1 can (15½ ounces) chestnut purée (unsweetened)
1 teaspoon vanilla extract
½ cup raisins
⅓ cup brandy
2 Delicious (red) apples
1 cup heavy cream, whipped
4 egg whites, beaten stiff

In a medium saucepan, lightly beat the egg yolks with the salt and milk. Sprinkle the gelatin over the yolk-milk mixture and let stand for 5 minutes to soften. Place over medium-low heat, constantly stirring, until the mixture coats the back of a spoon. Do not allow the mixture to boil; remove from heat.

Strain the syrup from the marron pieces into a measuring cup. Add honey to the syrup to make ½ cup. Stir the honey-syrup into the hot mixture. Add the chestnut purée and beat with a rotary or electric beater until smooth and well blended. Add the vanilla extract. Chill until slightly thickened.

Macerate the raisins in the brandy until the above mixture is thickened so that a mound forms when some mixture is dropped from a spoon. Whisk the mixture for 2 or 3 minutes. Whisk in the marron pieces, raisins, and brandy. Core the apples, but do not peel them. Chop them and add immediately to the gelatin mixture so that they do not turn brown. By hand, beat the mixture to make sure that all the ingredients are evenly distributed. Fold in the whipped cream. Fold in the stiffly beaten egg whites. Turn into the prepared mold and chill until set, preferably overnight.

Unmold, using Method 3.

This is delicious served with a roast turkey or chicken.

JELLIED CRANBERRY CREAM
(6-cup mold, lightly oiled)

1 envelope unflavored gelatin
¼ cup port wine
1½ cups water
2 cups sugar
4 cups fresh cranberries
1 tablespoon grated orange rind
1 cup sour cream

Soften the gelatin in the port wine. In a saucepan, combine the water and sugar, stirring until sugar is dissolved. Bring to a boil and add the cranberries. Simmer until cranberries pop, about 5 minutes. Remove from heat. Add the softened gelatin, stirring until gelatin is dissolved. Cool slightly.

Add the orange rind and sour cream, mixing well. Turn into the prepared mold and chill until set.

Unmold, using Method 3.

JELLIED CRANAPPLE FRUIT RELISH
(8-cup mold, dipped in cold water)

1 envelope unflavored gelatin
¼ cup port wine
1½ cups water
3 tablespoons lemon juice
2 cups sugar
4 cups fresh cranberries
1 cup white raisins
1 tablespoon grated lemon rind
3 tart apples
1 cup mandarin orange sections, drained

Soften the gelatin in the port wine. In a saucepan, combine the water, lemon juice, and sugar. Stir to dissolve the sugar. Bring to a boil and add the cranberries. Simmer until berries pop, about 5 minutes. Add the raisins and lemon rind. Simmer 2 minutes longer. Remove from heat. Add the softened gelatin, stirring until dissolved. Chill until cool and slightly set, stirring occasionally.

Core, peel, and dice the apples. Add the apples and oranges. Turn into the prepared mold and chill until set.

Unmold, using Method 1 or 2.

MOLDED HORSERADISH CREAM
(2½-cup mold, lightly oiled)

1 envelope unflavored gelatin
½ teaspoon salt
¼ cup cold water
⅓ cup prepared horseradish
¼ cup mayonnaise
1 cup sour cream
½ cup heavy cream, whipped

Sprinkle the gelatin and salt over the cold water in a small heat-resistant cup and let stand for 5 minutes to soften. Place cup in a pan of hot water over low heat, stirring until gelatin is dissolved. Combine the horseradish, mayonnaise, and sour cream. Add the dissolved gelatin. Fold in the whipped cream. Turn into the prepared mold and chill until set.

Unmold, using Method 3.

Serve with cold roast beef or other cold meats.

MUSTARD CREAM CUP
(1-cup mold, lightly oiled)

1½ teaspoons unflavored gelatin
2 tablespoons cold water
½ teaspoon lemon juice
1 tablespoon prepared mustard
  Dash of salt and pepper
½ cup mayonnaise
½ cup sour cream

In a small heat-resistant cup, sprinkle the gelatin over the combined water and lemon juice and let stand for 5 minutes to soften. Place cup in a pan of hot water over low heat, stirring until gelatin is dissolved. Combine with the remaining ingredients, mixing well. Turn into the prepared mold and chill until set.

Unmold, using Method 3.

Serve with cold meats.

MUSTARD MOUSSE
(4-cup mold, lightly oiled)

1 envelope unflavored gelatin
¼ cup white wine
2 egg yolks
½ cup sugar
⅛ teaspoon salt
2 tablespoons dry mustard
⅔ cup vinegar
⅓ cup water
1 cup heavy cream, whipped

Soften the gelatin in the white wine. In a small saucepan, lightly beat the egg yolks. Add the sugar, salt, and mustard.

Stir in the vinegar and water. Place over low heat, stirring until mixture begins to thicken slightly. (Do not boil.) Add the softened gelatin, stirring until gelatin is dissolved. Chill until slightly thickened and cool, stirring occasionally.

Beat the mixture until smooth and fluffy. Fold in the whipped cream. Turn into the prepared mold and chill until set.

Unmold, using Method 3.

Serve with cold meats.

ORANGE-APPLESAUCE RING
(2½-cup ring mold, dipped in cold water)

1 envelope unflavored gelatin
¼ cup orange juice
1 tablespoon sugar
1 jar (1 pound) applesauce or 2 cups homemade applesauce
1 tablespoon grated orange rind
1 teaspoon cinnamon

Sprinkle the gelatin over the orange juice in a small heat-resistant cup and let stand for 5 minutes to soften. Add the sugar. Place cup in a pan of hot water over low heat, stirring until gelatin and sugar are dissolved. Combine the applesauce, orange rind, and cinnamon. Add the dissolved gelatin. Turn into the prepared mold and chill until set.

Unmold, using Method 1 or 2.

Serve with pork or poultry.

TARTAR SAUCE MOUSSE
(2½-cup mold, lightly oiled)

1 envelope unflavored gelatin
¼ cup cold water
1 tablespoon lemon juice
1 teaspoon sugar
1 cup mayonnaise
⅓ cup sweet pickle relish
1 tablespoon capers, minced
½ cup heavy cream, whipped

In a small heat-resistant cup, soften the gelatin in the cold water. Add the lemon juice and sugar. Place cup in a pan of hot water over low heat, stirring until gelatin is dissolved. Combine the mayonnaise, relish, and capers. Stir in the dissolved gelatin. Fold in the whipped cream. Turn into the prepared mold and chill until set.

Unmold, using Method 3.

Serve with cold fish.

DESSERTS

Molded desserts are surely the most elegant finale to any meal. They are easy to prepare and can be made ahead of time. Leftovers will keep very well in the refrigerator for days, but be sure to cover them so that they do not absorb other food odors. The recipes in this chapter will delight every age group. Serve them for any special occasion or as desserts for your family meals. They go over great at any time.

ALMOND BAVARIAN WITH MACAROONS

(8-cup charlotte mold or straight-sided soufflé dish, lightly oiled)

    2 envelopes unflavored gelatin
    2 cups cold milk
    1-inch vanilla bean (optional)
    5 eggs, separated
    ½ cup sugar
    ½ cup Amaretto
    1 cup heavy cream, whipped

In a small saucepan, sprinkle the gelatin over the milk and let stand for 5 minutes to soften. Add the vanilla bean and, stirring, scald by bringing just to a boil. Remove from heat.

In another small saucepan, lightly beat the egg yolks with the sugar. Gradually add the hot milk. Over low heat, cook while stirring constantly until the mixture thickens slightly and coats the back of a spoon. Do not boil. Remove from heat; discard vanilla bean. Cool slightly.

Stir in the Amaretto. Chill until slightly thickened, stirring occasionally.

Beat the egg whites until stiff but not dry. Fold the whipped cream into the gelatin mixture; fold in the egg whites. Turn into the prepared mold and chill until set.

Unmold, using Method 3. Completely cover the top and garnish the sides of the Bavarian with Almond Macaroons (below).

ALMOND MACAROONS

(Yield: approximately 3 dozen)

    1 cup confectioners' sugar
    ⅛ teaspoon salt

8 ounces almond paste,* diced
1 tablespoon apricot preserves
2 egg whites, slightly beaten
1 teaspoon vanilla extract
Granulated sugar

Preheat the oven to 300°F. Line a cookie sheet with parchment paper.

In a large mixing bowl, using fingers, work the sugar and salt into the almond paste. Work in the preserves; gradually work in the egg whites. Add the vanilla.

Drop by rounded teaspoonfuls onto the prepared cookie sheet, 2 inches apart. Using your fingers, wet the tops of the cookies with water. Sprinkle on some granulated sugar. Bake at 300°F. for about 25 minutes, or until golden. Cool for 2 minutes; then with a spatula, remove to a wire rack to cool completely. Store in an airtight container.

FRESH APPLE MOUSSE
(6-cup mold, lightly oiled)

1 envelope unflavored gelatin
¼ cup cold water
½ cup apple juice
1 teaspoon grated lemon rind
2 tablespoons lemon juice
¾ cup sugar, extra-fine granulated
3 red eating apples
1 cup heavy cream, whipped

---

* When buying almond paste, gently squeeze the package with your fingertips to make sure the paste is pliable. When fresh, it should give slightly under a small amount of pressure.

Sprinkle the gelatin over the cold water in a heat-resistant cup and let stand for 5 minutes to soften. Place cup in a pan of hot water over low heat, stirring until gelatin is dissolved. Add to the apple juice. Add the lemon rind and juice. Add the sugar, stirring until it is dissolved. Chill until slightly thickened.

Using the largest hole of a grater, grate the apples, including the skin, directly into the thickened gelatin. (Note: Do not grate the core.) Fold in the whipped cream. Turn into the prepared mold and chill until set.

Unmold, using Method 3.

FRESH APPLESAUCE MOUSSE
(6-cup mold, lightly oiled)

3 tablespoons butter
6 cooking apples, cored and diced
1 tablespoon grated lemon rind
2 tablespoons honey
¼ cup brown sugar
1 envelope unflavored gelatin
¼ cup cold water
1 tablespoon lemon juice
1 cup heavy cream, whipped
Cinnamon

Melt the butter in a medium-sized saucepan. Add the apples and cook over low heat until they become very soft and pulpy. Force the cooked apples through a sieve or food mill. Add the lemon rind, honey, and brown sugar to the hot applesauce, mixing well until the sugar and honey are dissolved. Set aside to cool, stirring occasionally.

In a small heat-resistant cup, sprinkle the gelatin over the combined water and lemon juice and let stand for 5 minutes to soften. Place cup in a pan of hot water over low heat, stirring until gelatin is dissolved. Add to the applesauce. Chill until slightly thickened.

Fold in the whipped cream. Turn into the prepared mold and chill until set.

Unmold, using Method 3. Sprinkle with cinnamon.

APRICOT JELLY ROLL MOUSSE
(6-cup mixing bowl or 6-cup soufflé dish or charlotte mold, lined completely with plastic wrap)

JELLY ROLL

¾ cup flour
⅛ teaspoon salt
¾ teaspoon baking powder
3 large eggs
⅔ cup granulated sugar
1 teaspoon vanilla extract
¼ cup water
Confectioners' sugar
¾ cup apricot preserves

Preheat oven to 375°F. Grease a jelly roll pan, 17¼ x 11½ inches. Line with waxed paper and grease the paper.

Combine the flour, salt, and baking powder. Stir until well mixed; then sift once to remove any lumps.

In a medium-sized mixing bowl, beat the eggs on high speed for about 5 minutes, or until very thick. Gradually beat in the sugar until mixture makes a ribbon trail. On low speed, blend in the vanilla and water. Add the flour mixture all at once, beating just until smooth. Pour into the prepared pan, spreading the batter evenly and well into the corners.

Bake for 12 to 15 minutes, or until the cake is *lightly*

browned around the edges and firm to touch in the center. Do not overbake or it will crack when rolled.

Immediately loosen the edges of the cake and turn out onto a clean dish towel sprinkled with confectioners' sugar. Carefully remove the paper lining. Trim the stiff edges (about ¼ inch in) with a sharp knife. Spread the preserves evenly over the hot cake. Starting at the narrow end, tightly roll the cake, jelly-roll-fashion. Place seam side down and cool roll on a wire rack. Wrap and chill until ready for use.

APRICOT MOUSSE FILLING

4 ripe apricots, halved and pitted
1 cup water
¼ cup apricot preserves
2 egg yolks
⅓ cup sugar
1 envelope unflavored gelatin
¼ cup apricot brandy
1 cup heavy cream, whipped

Poach the apricot halves in the water for 10 to 15 minutes. Stir in the apricot preserves. Place apricot mixture in a blender and purée.

In a mixing bowl, lightly beat the egg yolks with the sugar. Add a small amount of the hot purée to the egg-yolk mixture. While stirring constantly, add the remaining purée.

Soften the gelatin in the apricot brandy for 5 minutes. Add to the hot purée and stir until gelatin is dissolved. If the purée has cooled, warm it over low heat, stirring constantly, until the gelatin dissolves. Do not let the mixture boil. Remove from heat and chill until slightly thickened, stirring occasionally.

Fold the whipped cream into the cooled apricot mixture.

TO ASSEMBLE

Line the 6-cup bowl with plastic wrap. Using a sharp knife, cut the jelly roll into 1/4-inch slices. Starting at the bottom of the bowl, line with jelly roll slices, pressing them together as closely as possible. Ladle the apricot mousse mixture into the center, being careful not to disarrange the jelly roll slices. Chill, covered, until set.

To unmold, simply turn over onto serving plate. Do not remove the plastic wrap until ready to serve as it will keep the jelly roll slices fresh.

Serve with cold Custard Sauce (below).

CUSTARD SAUCE
(Yield: 2 cups)

3 egg yolks
6 tablespoons sugar
1/4 teaspoon salt
2 cups half-and-half, warmed
1 1/2 teaspoons vanilla extract

In the top of a double boiler, lightly beat the egg yolks with the sugar and salt. Gradually add the half-and-half and, stirring constantly, cook over hot water until mixture coats a spoon. Do not boil. Stir in the vanilla. Cover with plastic wrap while hot to prevent a skin from forming. Chill, covered.

BLACKBERRY-AND-APPLE MOUSSE
(6-cup mold, lightly oiled)

> 1 pint blackberries, washed
> ½ cup water
> 1 envelope plus 1½ teaspoons unflavored gelatin
> ¼ cup blackberry brandy
> Sugar to taste
> 2 egg yolks
> 2 tablespoons sugar
> 1 cup milk, scalded
> 1 Delicious (red) apple, cored
> 1 cup heavy cream, whipped

In a small saucepan, combine the blackberries and water and simmer for 5 minutes. Strain to remove seeds.

Soften gelatin in blackberry brandy for 5 minutes. Add to the hot strained blackberry purée. Add sugar to taste and stir until gelatin and sugar are dissolved.

In the top of a double boiler, beat the egg yolks with the 2 tablespoons sugar. Place over hot (not boiling) water over low heat and gradually add the milk, stirring constantly, until mixture begins to thicken. Remove from heat. Stir in the blackberry purée. Chill until slightly thickened.

Peel the apple and grate directly into the chilled mixture. Fold in the whipped cream. Turn into the prepared mold and chill until set.

Unmold, using Method 3.

PORTED BLUEBERRY MOUSSE
(4-cup mold, lightly oiled)

> 1 envelope unflavored gelatin
> ¼ cup port wine

2 egg yolks
⅓ cup sugar
1 cup milk, scalded
1 pint fresh blueberries, washed and picked over
1 cup heavy cream, whipped

Soften the gelatin in the port wine. In a saucepan, lightly beat the egg yolks with the sugar. Gradually add the hot milk. Place over low heat and cook, stirring constantly, until the mixture thickens very slightly. (Do not boil.) Remove from heat. Stir in the softened gelatin until it is dissolved. Chill until slightly thickened, stirring occasionally.

Gently fold in the blueberries and whipped cream. Turn into the prepared mold and chill until set.

Unmold, using Method 3.

CARAMEL MOUSSE
(4-cup mold, lightly oiled)

¾ cup sugar
¾ cup water, divided
1 envelope unflavored gelatin
1¼ cups cold milk, divided
3 egg yolks
2 tablespoons sugar
¼ teaspoon vanilla extract
½ cup heavy cream, whipped

In a small but deep saucepan, combine the ¾ cup sugar with ¼ cup of water. Heat and let boil until golden brown. Do not stir, but give the pan an occasional swirl during the boiling process. Be very watchful when the color begins to turn golden, for the mixture will burn if you do not take the pan *off the burner* the moment the mixture reaches the correct color.

Wrap a towel around the hand holding the pan and add the remaining ½ cup of water. Stand back as far away as possible when doing this, as the added water will sizzle and splash. The towel is to protect your hand from any splashes. After the addition of the water, replace the pan on the burner over low heat, stirring until the mixture is smooth. Be sure to scrape the bottom of the pan, as the caramel hardens when the cold water is added.

Sprinkle the gelatin over ¼ cup of cold milk and let stand to soften. In another small saucepan, lightly beat the egg yolks with the 2 tablespoons sugar. Add the vanilla and the remaining 1 cup cold milk. Place over medium heat, stirring constantly, until the custard begins to thicken. Do not boil or the custard will curdle. Add the softened gelatin to the hot custard and stir until gelatin is dissolved.

If necessary, reheat the caramel, stirring until it is smooth. Add to the hot custard, mixing well. Cool slightly and then chill until slightly thickened, stirring occasionally. If you do not stir, the mixture will get lumpy.

Fold in the whipped cream. Turn into the prepared mold and chill until set.

Unmold, using Method 3.

CHARLOTTE BUTTER CREAM
(6-cup charlotte mold, prepared as instructed on page 12)

3 eggs, separated
½ cup sugar, divided
1 cup cold milk
1 envelope unflavored gelatin
2 ounces cream cheese, softened and diced
½ teaspoon imitation butter flavoring
1 cup heavy cream, whipped
1 package ladyfingers
Pecan halves (for garnish)
Semisweet chocolate morsels or shaved curls (for garnish)

In a medium-sized saucepan, lightly beat the egg yolks with ¼ cup of sugar and the cold milk. Sprinkle the gelatin over the mixture and let stand for 5 minutes to soften. Place over low heat, stirring constantly, until mixture coats the back of a spoon. Add the cream cheese and whisk or beat until smooth. Remove from heat before mixture starts to boil. Cool slightly.

Add the butter flavoring. Chill until cold and slightly thickened, stirring occasionally.

Beat the egg whites until frothy. Gradually add the remaining ¼ cup of sugar and continue beating until stiff but not dry. Beat the thickened custard until smooth. Fold in the whipped cream. Fold in the egg whites.

Line the sides of the mold with the ladyfingers (rounded side out). Turn the mixture into the prepared mold and chill until set.

Unmold, using Method 6. Remove waxed paper before serving. Garnish with pecan halves and chocolate morsels or curls.

CHARLOTTE RUSSE AU GRAND MARNIER
(4-cup charlotte mold, prepared as instructed on page 12)

4 egg yolks
½ cup sugar
1 cup milk, scalded
1 envelope unflavored gelatin
¼ cup orange juice
¼ cup Grand Marnier
1 cup heavy cream, whipped
1 package ladyfingers

In a small saucepan, lightly beat the egg yolks with the sugar. Gradually beat in the scalded milk. Cook over low heat, stirring constantly, until the mixture thickens slightly and coats the back of a spoon. Do not let the mixture boil. Remove from heat.

Soften the gelatin in the orange juice. Add it to the hot custard, stirring until gelatin is dissolved. Cool slightly.

Whisk in the Grand Marnier. Chill until slightly thickened, stirring occasionally.

Fold in the whipped cream. Line the sides of the mold with the ladyfingers (rounded side out). Turn the mixture into the prepared mold and chill until set.

Unmold, using Method 6.

Note: This recipe may be doubled.

DOUBLE CHEESE BAVARIAN
(8-cup mold, lightly oiled)

2 envelopes unflavored gelatin
1 cup cold milk
2 eggs, separated

1 cup sugar
½ teaspoon salt
1 package (8 ounces) cream cheese, diced
2 teaspoons grated lemon rind
2 tablespoons lemon juice
2 cups ricotta cheese
1 cup heavy cream, whipped

Soften the gelatin in the milk for 5 minutes. In the top of a double boiler, beat the egg yolks with the sugar and salt. Add the gelatin milk. Place over hot, not boiling, water, stirring until the mixture begins to thicken. Add the cream cheese, stirring until melted. Cool.

Combine the lemon rind and juice with the ricotta cheese. Add the cooled custard, mixing well. Chill slightly.

Beat the egg whites until stiff. Fold the whipped cream into the cheese mixture. Fold in the egg whites. Turn into the prepared mold and chill until set.

Unmold, using Method 3.

BRANDIED CHESTNUT BAVARIAN
(8-cup mold, lightly oiled)

4 eggs, separated
1½ cups cold milk
1 envelope plus 1 teaspoon unflavored gelatin
⅔ cup honey
1 can (15½ ounces) chestnut purée (unsweetened)
1 teaspoon vanilla extract
½ cup brandy
1 cup heavy cream, whipped
1 jar (10 ounces) whole marrons in syrup (for garnish; optional)
Heavy cream, whipped (for garnish; optional)

In a medium saucepan, lightly beat the egg yolks with the milk. Sprinkle the gelatin over the milk and let stand for 5 minutes to soften. Place over low-medium heat, stirring constantly, until the mixture coats the back of a spoon. Stir in the honey. Do not allow mixture to boil. Remove from heat. Add the chestnut purée and beat with a rotary or electric beater until smooth. Cool slightly.

Add the vanilla extract and brandy. Chill until slightly thickened, stirring occasionally. (The mixture will form a mound when dropped from a spoon.)

Beat the chilled mixture for 2 to 3 minutes. Beat the egg whites until stiff but not dry. Fold the whipped cream into the thickened mixture, then fold in the beaten egg whites. Turn into the prepared mold and chill until set, preferably overnight.

Unmold, using Method 3. Garnish with the whole marrons and additional whipped cream, if desired.

Note: This makes a very different but excellent winter holiday dessert.

DOUBLE CHOCOLATE PINWHEEL
(8-cup mixing bowl or 8-cup soufflé dish or charlotte mold, lined completely with plastic wrap)

CHOCOLATE JELLY ROLL

    ¾ cup flour
    ¾ teaspoon baking powder
    ⅛ teaspoon salt
    2 tablespoons cocoa
    3 large eggs
    1 cup granulated sugar
    1 teaspoon vanilla extract
    ¼ cup water
    1 recipe Stabilized Frosting Cream (page 145)

Preheat oven to 375°F. Grease a jelly roll pan, 17¼ x 11½ inches. Line with waxed paper and grease the paper.

Combine the flour, baking powder, salt, and cocoa. Stir until well mixed; then sift once to remove any lumps.

In a medium-sized mixing bowl, beat the eggs on high speed for about 5 minutes, or until very thick. Gradually beat in the sugar until mixture makes a ribbon trail. On low speed, blend in the vanilla and water. Add the flour mixture all at once, beating just until smooth. Pour into the prepared pan, spreading the batter evenly and well into the corners.

Bake for 12 to 15 minutes, or until the cake is *lightly* browned around the edges and firm to touch in the center. Do not overbake or it will crack when rolled.

Immediately loosen the edges of the cake and turn out onto a clean dish towel sprinkled with confectioners' sugar. Carefully remove the paper lining. Trim the stiff edges (about ¼ inch in) with a sharp knife. While hot, tightly roll the cake and towel together, jelly-roll-fashion, starting at the narrow end. Cool wrapped cake on a wire rack.

When cool, unroll cake; remove towel. Spread the Stabilized Frosting Cream on the unrolled cake. You will use only about ¾ cup of filling. Using a decorating tube, pipe whipped cream decorations onto a cookie sheet and freeze for garnish. Tightly reroll the cake. Wrap and chill until ready for use.

CHOCOLATE FILLING

    3 1-ounce squares unsweetened chocolate
    ½ cup cold water, divided
    1 envelope unflavored gelatin
    4 eggs, separated
    ¾ cup sugar, divided
    ¼ cup brandy, rum, or orange-flavored liqueur
    1 cup heavy cream, whipped

In the top of a double boiler, melt chocolate with ¼ cup water, over hot water in bottom of boiler. Soften the gelatin in the remaining ¼ cup of water. Add the softened gelatin to the melted chocolate, stirring until gelatin is dissolved.

In a mixing bowl, beat egg yolks with ½ cup of sugar until very thick, about 5 minutes. Beat in the brandy. Gradually stir the chocolate mixture into the egg-yolk mixture. Fold in the whipped cream. Beat the egg whites until frothy. Add the remaining sugar (¼ cup) and continue beating until stiff peaks form. Fold into the chocolate mixture.

TO ASSEMBLE

Line the 8-cup bowl with plastic wrap. Using a sharp knife, cut the chocolate jelly roll into ¼-inch slices. Starting at the bottom of the bowl, line with jelly roll slices, pressing them together as closely as possible. Ladle the chocolate filling into the center, being careful not to disarrange the jelly roll slices. Chill, covered, until set.

To unmold, simply turn over onto serving plate. Do not remove the plastic wrap until ready to serve as it will keep the jelly roll slices fresh. Garnish with frozen whipped cream decorations. Any leftover cake slices may also be used as a garnish around the platter.

COCONUT BAVARIAN CREAM
(4-cup mold, lightly oiled)

1 envelope unflavored gelatin
¼ cup cold milk
3 egg yolks
⅛ teaspoon salt
¾ cup sweetened cream of coconut
1 cup milk
2 egg whites

½ cup heavy cream, whipped
Shredded coconut (for garnish; optional)

Soften the gelatin in ¼ cup cold milk. In a saucepan, lightly beat the egg yolks, salt, cream of coconut, and 1 cup milk. Cook over low heat, stirring constantly, until mixture thickens slightly and coats the back of a spoon. (Do not boil.) Remove from heat. Add the softened gelatin to the hot custard and stir until gelatin is dissolved. Set aside to cool, stirring occasionally to prevent a skin from forming on the surface. Chill until slightly thickened.

Beat the egg whites until stiff. Beat the slightly thickened custard until smooth. Fold the whipped cream into the custard. Fold in the egg whites. Turn into the prepared mold and chill until set.

Unmold, using Method 3. Garnish with shredded coconut, if desired.

COFFEE RICOTTA BAVARIAN
(6-cup mold, lightly oiled)

1 envelope unflavored gelatin
1 cup strong black coffee, cold
½ cup sugar
1½ cups ricotta cheese
3 tablespoons coffee-flavored liqueur
2 egg whites
1 cup heavy cream, whipped

In a small saucepan, sprinkle the gelatin over the coffee and let stand for 5 minutes to soften. Add the sugar. Place over low heat, stirring constantly, until gelatin is dissolved. Combine the cheese and the liqueur. Add the coffee. Beat until well mixed. Chill until slightly thickened.

Beat the egg whites until stiff. Fold the whipped cream into the cheese mixture. Fold in the egg whites. Turn into the prepared mold and chill until set.

Unmold, using Method 3.

Serve with chocolate sauce.

FIG MOUSSE
(6-cup mold, lightly oiled)

2 envelopes unflavored gelatin
½ cup cold water
2 cans (12 ounces each) pear nectar, chilled
½ cup cream sherry
1 can or jar (approximately 16 ounces) figs in syrup
1 cup heavy cream, whipped

In a small heat-resistant cup, sprinkle the gelatin over the water and let stand for 5 minutes to soften. Place cup in a pan of hot water over low heat, stirring constantly until gelatin is dissolved.

In a large mixing bowl, combine the dissolved gelatin with the nectar and sherry. Drain the figs and add the syrup to the mixture. Chill until slightly thickened, stirring occasionally.

Beat with a rotary or electric beater about 5 minutes, or until frothy. Cut the figs in half and fold into the mixture. Fold in the whipped cream. Turn into the prepared mold and chill until set.

Unmold, using Method 3.

GINGER MOUSSE
(4-cup mold, lightly oiled)

  2 eggs, separated
  1/3 cup sugar
  1 envelope unflavored gelatin
  1 cup cold milk, divided
  1/8 teaspoon salt
  2 tablespoons rum or brandy
  1/2 cup finely chopped preserved ginger
  1 cup heavy cream, whipped

In the top of a double boiler, beat the egg yolks with the sugar. Soften the gelatin in 1/4 cup of cold milk. Gradually add the remaining 3/4 cup cold milk to the egg yolks, cooking over hot (not boiling) water until the mixture coats the back of a metal spoon. Add the softened gelatin, stirring until gelatin is dissolved. Add the salt and chill until cool and almost set, stirring occasionally.

Add the rum or brandy and the ginger to the thickened gelatin. Beat the egg whites until stiff. Fold the whipped cream into the custard. Fold in the egg whites. Turn into the prepared mold and chill until set.

Unmold, using Method 3.

FRESH LEMON OR LIME SNOW PUDDING
(6-cup mold, dipped in cold water)

  1 envelope unflavored gelatin
  1 1/2 cups cold water, divided
  1 cup sugar
  1/4 teaspoon salt
  2 teaspoons grated lemon or lime rind
  1/4 cup fresh lemon or lime juice
  3 egg whites, *un*beaten

In a small saucepan, sprinkle gelatin over ½ cup cold water and let stand for 5 minutes to soften. Place over low heat, stirring constantly, until gelatin is dissolved. Remove from heat. Add sugar and salt; stir until they are dissolved. Transfer to a large mixing bowl. Stir in the remaining 1 cup cold water, rind, and juice. Chill until slightly thickened, stirring occasionally.

Add the unbeaten egg whites. Using an electric mixer, beat at high speed for about 10 minutes, or until the mixture is fluffy and thick enough to hold its shape. Turn into the prepared mold and chill until set.

Unmold, using Method 1 or 2.

Serve with fruit, Custard Sauce (page 161), or whipped cream.

LAYERED LEMON-AND-LIME MOUSSE
(8-cup mold, lightly oiled)

LEMON LAYER

    1 envelope unflavored gelatin
    ¼ cup lemon juice
    2 egg yolks
    ½ cup sugar
    1¼ cups milk, scalded
    1 tablespoon grated lemon rind
    Yellow food coloring
    ¾ cup heavy cream, whipped

LIME LAYER

    1 envelope unflavored gelatin
    ¼ cup lime juice
    2 egg yolks
    ½ cup sugar

1¼ cups milk, scalded
1 tablespoon grated lime rind
Green food coloring
¾ cup heavy cream, whipped

The two layers must be made separately. The directions below apply to each.

Soften the gelatin in the juice for 5 minutes. In the top of a double boiler, lightly beat the egg yolks with the sugar. Place in a pan of hot (not boiling) water over low heat, stirring constantly. Gradually add the milk and continue stirring until the mixture coats the back of a spoon. Remove from heat. Add the rind. Add the softened gelatin, stirring until gelatin is dissolved. Chill until slightly thickened and cool, stirring occasionally.

Add a few drops of food coloring. Fold the whipped cream into one layer. Turn this into the prepared mold and chill until very thick but not completely set.

Fold the whipped cream into the second layer. Pour on top of the layer that is nearly set. Chill until completely set.

Unmold, using Method 3.

MACÉDOINE MOUSSE OF FRESH FRUITS
(6-cup mold, lightly oiled)

1 envelope unflavored gelatin
1 cup orange juice
½ cup sugar
1 tablespoon grated lemon rind
¼ cup kirsch
1 cup sour cream
2 tangerines, peeled and sectioned
2 ripe pears, peeled and diced
2 ripe peaches, peeled and diced
½ pound seedless green grapes
1 ripe banana, peeled and sliced
½ cup heavy cream, whipped

Note: Do not cut the fruit until the gelatin is slightly thickened. At that point, you may prepare the fruit and add it directly to the mixture, stirring with each addition. This will prevent the fruit from discoloring.

Sprinkle the gelatin over the orange juice in a small saucepan and let stand for 5 minutes to soften. Add the sugar and heat, stirring until gelatin is dissolved. Add the grated lemon rind and cool.

Stir in the kirsch and sour cream. Chill until slightly thickened.

Prepare the fresh fruit and stir each into the thickened gelatin. Fold in the whipped cream. Turn into the prepared mold and chill until set.

Unmold, using Method 3.

MALTAISE RICE MOUSSE
(5-cup mold, lightly oiled)

1 cup long-grain rice, raw
2½ cups milk, scalded
1 teaspoon vanilla extract
⅛ teaspoon salt
3 tablespoons grated orange rind
1 envelope unflavored gelatin
¼ cup orange-flavored liqueur
1 egg yolk
½ cup sugar
¾ cup cold milk
¾ cup heavy cream, whipped
Garnish (see below)

In a saucepan, combine the rice, milk, vanilla, salt, and orange rind. Cover and simmer very gently for 30 minutes, or until soft and creamy. Cool slightly.

Soften the gelatin in the orange-flavored liqueur. In another saucepan, lightly beat the egg yolk with the sugar. Add the cold milk, mixing well. Cook over low heat, stirring constantly, until mixture thickens slightly and coats the back of a spoon. (Do not boil.) Remove from heat. Add the softened gelatin, stirring until gelatin is dissolved. Add to the rice mixture. Chill until cool and slightly thickened, stirring occasionally.

Fold in the whipped cream. Turn into the prepared mold and chill until set.

Unmold, using Method 3. Garnish as below.

For garnish, heat until liquid ½ cup red currant jelly and 1 teaspoon orange juice. Cool slightly.

Peel and section 2 small navel oranges. Using a toothpick, dip sections in the melted jelly. Place in a pattern on top of the turned-out mousse.

MAPLE MOUSSE
(4-cup mold, lightly oiled)

3 egg yolks
1 envelope unflavored gelatin
1/4 teaspoon salt
1 cup cold milk
2/3 cup maple syrup
1 tablespoon rum
1 cup heavy cream, whipped

In a medium-sized saucepan, lightly beat the egg yolks with the gelatin and salt. Add the cold milk and place over low heat, stirring constantly, until mixture begins to thicken. (Do not boil.) Add the maple syrup and continue stirring until smooth and well blended. Turn off the heat and add the rum. Cool and then chill until slightly thickened.

Fold in the whipped cream. Turn into the prepared mold and chill until set.

Unmold, using Method 3.

NESSELRODE RICOTTA BAVARIAN
(6-cup mold, lightly oiled)

1 envelope unflavored gelatin
1 cup cold milk
1/2 cup sugar
1 teaspoon almond extract
1 1/2 cups ricotta cheese
3 tablespoons rum
1/2 cup of bottled nesselrode mix
2 egg whites
1 cup heavy cream, whipped

In a small saucepan, sprinkle the gelatin over the milk and let stand for 5 minutes to soften. Add the sugar. Place over low heat, stirring until gelatin and sugar are dissolved. Remove from heat. Add the almond extract. Combine the cheese and the rum. Add the milk mixture. Beat until well blended. Chill until slightly thickened.

Add the nesselrode mix. Beat the egg whites until stiff. Fold the whipped cream into the nesselrode-cheese mixture. Fold in the egg whites. Turn into the prepared mold and chill until set.

Unmold, using Method 3.

Serve with chocolate sauce.

ORANGE-CHERRY BAVARIAN CREAM
(4-cup mold, lightly oiled)

1 envelope unflavored gelatin
1/2 cup cold water
1/2 cup sugar
1 cup orange juice
1/4 cup lemon juice
2 egg whites at room temperature
1/2 cup heavy cream, whipped
Cherry Sauce (below)
Green Almond Leaves (below)
Fresh dark sweet cherries, pitted

In a small saucepan, sprinkle gelatin over cold water and let stand 5 minutes to soften. Add the sugar and heat over a medium fire, gently stirring until dissolved. Cool slightly, then add the fruit juices. Chill until slightly thickened, stirring occasionally.

Beat the egg whites until stiff but not dry. Fold the

whipped cream, then the egg whites, into the chilled gelatin mixture. Turn into the prepared mold and chill until set.

Unmold, using Method 3. Pour the Cherry Sauce over the top and decorate with Green Almond Leaves and fresh cherries.

CHERRY SAUCE

Halve and pit about 2 cups fresh dark sweet cherries (this can be done earlier). Shortly before serving, mix with light corn syrup and sugar to taste.

GREEN ALMOND LEAVES

Mix an 8-ounce package of almond paste with enough sugar to the right consistency for rolling. Add a little green food coloring. Roll out on waxed paper to about ⅛ inch thick. Using a pastry wheel, cut out into the shape of leaves and make veins with a knife. Place the leaves side by side over the rolling pin to shape in a slight curve and dry. Store in an airtight container.

PAPAYA MOUSSE
(4-cup mold, lightly oiled)

> 5 cups peeled, seeded, and cubed papaya
> 1⅔ cups water, divided
> 1 cup sugar
> ⅔ cup lime or lemon juice
> 1¼ teaspoons ground ginger
> ½ teaspoon vanilla extract
> 1 envelope plus 1 teaspoon unflavored gelatin
> 1 cup heavy cream, whipped
> 1 lime, sliced (for garnish; optional)
> Heavy cream, whipped (for garnish; optional)

In a medium saucepan, combine the papaya, 1⅓ cups water, and sugar. Bring to a boil while stirring constantly. Lower heat; cover and simmer for 10 minutes. Add the lime juice and ginger; simmer 5 minutes longer. Remove from heat; stir in the vanilla. Measure out 2 cups of this sauce; cover and store the remainder in the refrigerator.

In a small heat-resistant cup, soften the gelatin in the remaining ⅓ cup of water for 5 minutes. Place cup in a pan of hot water over low heat, gently stirring until gelatin is dissolved. Stir the dissolved gelatin into the 2 cups of papaya sauce. Chill until slightly thickened, stirring occasionally.

Fold in the whipped cream. Turn into the prepared mold and chill until set.

Unmold, using Method 3.

To serve, pour the remaining papaya sauce over the mold. Garnish with lime slices and additional whipped cream, if desired.

PEAR NECTAR BAVARIAN
(4-cup mold, lightly oiled)

1 envelope unflavored gelatin
1 can (8¼ ounces) Bartlett pear halves, drained
¼ cup liquid drained from pears, add water if necessary
1 can (12 ounces) pear nectar
1 tablespoon grated lemon rind
2 tablespoons sugar
½ teaspoon vanilla extract
1 cup heavy cream, whipped

In a small heat-resistant cup, sprinkle the gelatin on the ¼ cup liquid drained from the pears and let stand for 5 minutes to soften. Place cup in a pan of hot water over low heat, stirring until gelatin is dissolved. Add to the pear nectar. Add the lemon rind and sugar, mixing well. Add the vanilla extract. Chill until slightly thickened but not set.

Beat until smooth and fluffy. Fold in the whipped cream. Turn into the prepared mold and chill until set.

Unmold, using Method 3. Garnish with the pear halves.

Variations

Apricot Nectar Bavarian

Substitute 1 can (8¼ ounces) apricot halves for the Bartlett pear halves and 1 can (12 ounces) apricot nectar for the pear nectar.

Peach Nectar Bavarian

Substitute 1 can (8¼ ounces) peach halves for the Bartlett pear halves and 1 can (12 ounces) peach nectar for the pear nectar.

PINEAPPLE CHARLOTTE
(8-cup charlotte mold, prepared as instructed on page 12)

> 2 envelopes unflavored gelatin
> 1 can (20 ounces) crushed pineapple in heavy syrup, drained (reserve syrup)*
> 4 eggs, separated
> 1 cup milk
> ½ cup sugar, divided
> ½ teaspoon vanilla extract
> 1 cup heavy cream, whipped
> 1 package ladyfingers

Soften the gelatin in the syrup drained from the pineapple. In a small saucepan, lightly beat the egg yolks. Add the milk

* Do not use fresh or frozen pineapple for this dish as both contain an enzyme that resists the jelling process.

and ¼ cup of sugar, mixing well. Cook over low heat, stirring constantly, until the mixture coats the back of a spoon. Remove from heat. Add the softened gelatin, stirring until gelatin is dissolved. Stir in the vanilla extract. Chill until slightly thickened, stirring occasionally.

Stir in the crushed pineapple. (Reserve ¼ cup of the crushed pineapple for garnish, if desired.) Beat the egg whites until frothy. Gradually add the remaining ¼ cup of sugar, beating until stiff but not dry. Fold in the whipped cream. Fold in the beaten egg whites. Line the charlotte mold with the ladyfingers. Turn the mixture into the prepared mold. Chill until set.

Unmold, using Method 6. Carefully remove waxed paper before serving.

PISTACHIO MOUSSE CHRISTMAS WREATH
(8-cup ring mold, lightly oiled)

8 egg yolks
1 cup sugar
2 cups milk, scalded
2 envelopes unflavored gelatin
¼ cup cold water
Green food coloring
½ teaspoon almond extract
½ cup Pistàshà liqueur
2 cups heavy cream, whipped
Candied cherries (for garnish)
Angelica (for garnish)

In the top of a double boiler, beat the egg yolks with the sugar. Gradually add the scalded milk. Cook over hot (not boiling) water, stirring constantly until thickened.

Soften the gelatin in the cold water. Add to the hot custard and stir until gelatin is dissolved. Set aside to cool, stirring occasionally to prevent a skin from forming on the surface.

Add enough green food coloring to achieve a shade slightly darker than the desired shade. Add the almond extract and the Pistàshà liqueur. Chill until slightly thickened.

Fold in the whipped cream. Turn into the prepared ring mold and chill until set.

Unmold, using Method 3. Decorate with candied cherries and angelica cut into holly leaf shapes.

MARBLED PLUM CHARLOTTE
(6-cup charlotte mold, prepared as instructed on page 12)

PLUM PUDDING

> 2 cans (17 ounces each) whole purple plums in heavy syrup
> 2 envelopes unflavored gelatin
> ½ cup orange juice
> ¼ cup sugar
> ¼ teaspoon cinnamon
> Red food coloring
> 1 package ladyfingers
> 8 whole almonds (for garnish; optional)

MARBLE

> 2 egg yolks
> ¼ cup sugar
> 1 teaspoon vanilla extract
> 1 envelope unflavored gelatin
> 2 cups cold milk

PLUM PUDDING

Drain the plums, reserving the syrup. Halve and pit the plums. Reserve 8 of the choicest halves for garnish. Place the remainder in a blender and purée.

Soften the gelatin in the orange juice. Place the plum syrup in a small saucepan with the sugar and cinnamon. Add the softened gelatin. Place over low heat, stirring constantly, until the sugar and gelatin are dissolved. Remove from heat. Stir in the plum purée and enough red food coloring to obtain the shade desired. Chill until slightly thickened, stirring occasionally.

MARBLE

In a small saucepan, lightly beat the egg yolks, sugar, vanilla, and gelatin. Add the cold milk, mixing well. Place over low heat, stirring constantly, until mixture thickens slightly and coats the back of a spoon. (Do not boil.) Remove from heat. Chill until slightly thickened, stirring occasionally.

TO ASSEMBLE

Line the sides of the charlotte mold with ladyfingers (rounded side out). Gently pour in the slightly thickened plum gelatin. Carefully pour the slightly thickened custard gelatin over the plum layer. Using a spoon or knife, swirl the custard through the plum gelatin to achieve a marbled effect. Chill until set.

Unmold, using Method 6. Garnish with the reserved plums. These may be stuffed with almonds, if desired.

MOLDED PRUNE WHIP
(6-cup mold, dipped in cold water)

    1 envelope unflavored gelatin
    1/4 cup orange juice or cold water
    1 3/4 cups prune juice
    1/2 teaspoon grated orange rind
    Sugar to taste
    2 egg whites, *un*beaten

Sprinkle the gelatin over the orange juice in a small heat-resistant cup and let stand for 5 minutes to soften. Place cup in a pan of hot water over low heat, stirring until gelatin is dissolved. Add to the prune juice, stirring well. Add the orange rind and sugar to taste. Chill until slightly thickened, stirring occasionally.

When nearly set, remove from refrigerator and beat until frothy. Add the unbeaten egg whites. Continue beating with an electric beater until fluffy and tripled in volume. Pour into the prepared mold and chill until set.

Unmold, using Method 1 or 2.

Serve with Custard Sauce (page 161) or light cream.

Variations

MOLDED CRANBERRY WHIP

Substitute 2 cups cranberry cocktail for the ¼ cup orange juice and 1¾ cups prune juice.

MOLDED NECTAR WHIP

Substitute 2 cups nectar (apricot, peach, or pear) for the ¼ cup orange juice and 1¾ cups prune juice.

PUMPKIN BAVARIAN—THANKSGIVING DAY DELIGHT
(6-cup mold, lightly oiled)

¾ cup soft brown sugar, firmly packed
½ teaspoon salt
½ teaspoon nutmeg
¼ teaspoon ginger
1 teaspoon cinnamon
2 eggs, separated

2 envelopes unflavored gelatin
1 cup cold milk
1 can (16 ounces) pumpkin
1 teaspoon vanilla extract
1 cup heavy cream, whipped
Additional whipped cream (for garnish)

In a small saucepan, combine the brown sugar, salt, nutmeg, ginger, cinnamon, egg yolks, gelatin, and milk. Beat slightly. Place over low heat and cook, stirring constantly, until the mixture coats the back of a spoon. (Do not boil.) Remove from heat.

In a large mixing bowl, combine the pumpkin and vanilla extract. Add the hot custard, mixing well. Chill until cold and slightly thickened, stirring occasionally.

Beat the egg whites until stiff but not dry. Beat the chilled pumpkin mixture until smooth. Fold in the whipped cream. Fold in the beaten egg whites. Turn into the prepared mold and chill until set.

Unmold, using Method 3. Garnish and serve with additional whipped cream.

EASY RASPBERRY BAVARIAN
(4-cup mold, lightly oiled)

1 package (3 ounces) raspberry-flavored gelatin
1 cup boiling water
1 package frozen raspberries, thawed and drained
Drained raspberry juice plus cold water to make 1 cup liquid
1/4 teaspoon vanilla extract
1/2 cup heavy cream, whipped

Dissolve the gelatin in the boiling water. Add the 1 cup of cold liquid (raspberry juice plus water). Stir well. Add the vanilla extract. Chill until slightly thickened but not set.

Beat until smooth and fluffy. Add the raspberries and fold in the whipped cream. Turn into the prepared mold and chill until set.

Unmold, using Method 3.

Variations

STRAWBERRY BAVARIAN

Substitute strawberry-flavored gelatin and use frozen strawberries instead of raspberries.

PINEAPPLE BAVARIAN

Substitute pineapple-flavored gelatin and use 1 can (8¼ ounces) crushed pineapple instead of raspberries.

PEACH BAVARIAN

Substitute peach-flavored gelatin and use 1 can (8½ ounces) sliced peaches, finely chopped, instead of raspberries.

FRESH RHUBARB MOUSSE
(4-cup mold, lightly oiled)

   1 pound fresh rhubarb, cut into ½- to ¾-inch pieces
   1 cup sugar
   ⅛ teaspoon cinnamon
   ⅛ teaspoon salt
   2 strips lemon peel
   1 strip orange peel
   ¼ cup water
   ¼ teaspoon vanilla extract
   1 envelope unflavored gelatin

¼ cup orange juice
1 cup heavy cream, whipped
Additional whipped cream (for garnish)
Red food coloring (optional)
Cinnamon (for garnish)

In a saucepan, combine the first 7 ingredients. Cover and bring to a boil. Turn down heat and simmer gently for 5 minutes. Remove the lemon and orange peel. Stir in the vanilla extract. Taste for sweetness; add more sugar, if necessary.

Soften the gelatin in the orange juice for 5 minutes. Stir into the hot rhubarb until gelatin is dissolved. Chill until slightly thickened, stirring occasionally.

Fold in the whipped cream. A few drops of red food coloring may be added if a deeper shade of pink is desired. Turn into the prepared mold and chill until set.

Unmold, using Method 3. Garnish with whipped cream sprinkled with cinnamon.

RIZ À L'IMPÉRATRICE
(6-cup mold, lightly oiled)

4 cups water
1 cup long-grain rice, raw
3 cups milk, divided
Grated rind of 1 orange
2½ teaspoons vanilla extract
¼ teaspoon salt
1 cup slivered glacéed fruit
2 tablespoons orange juice
4 egg yolks
½ cup sugar
2 tablespoons light rum
2 tablespoons cold water
1 envelope unflavored gelatin
1 cup heavy cream, whipped
Glacéed cherries (for garnish)

Bring the water to a boil in a medium-sized saucepan. Add the rice; bring to a boil again and cook for 2 minutes. Drain and return rice to the saucepan. Add 1½ cups milk, grated orange rind, vanilla, and salt. Cover and cook over very low heat about 30 minutes, or until the rice is tender and the liquid absorbed. (Additional milk may be added if the rice becomes too dry before it is soft.) Set aside.

Sprinkle the slivered fruit with the orange juice and set aside.

In a small saucepan, lightly beat the egg yolks with the sugar. Add the remaining 1½ cups of milk and cook over low heat, stirring constantly, until the mixture coats the back of a spoon. Remove from heat.

Combine the rum and cold water in a small cup. Add the gelatin and let stand for 5 minutes to soften.

Add the softened gelatin to the hot custard, stirring until dissolved. Taste for sweetness and add more sugar, if desired. Add the custard to the cooked rice, mixing well. Chill until cool and just beginning to set, stirring occasionally.

Stir in the macerated fruit, mixing well. Fold in the whipped cream. Turn into the prepared mold and chill until set.

Unmold, using Method 3. Garnish with the glacéed cherries.

ROSÉ SABAYON MOUSSE
(6-cup mold, lightly oiled)

> 6 egg yolks
> 1½ cups confectioners' sugar
> 2 cups rosé wine
> 2 envelopes unflavored gelatin
> 2 cups heavy cream, whipped
> Sugar-frosted grapes (for garnish; page 120)

In a small saucepan, lightly beat the egg yolks with the sugar. Add the wine. Sprinkle the gelatin over the mixture and let stand for 5 minutes to soften. Place over low heat and cook, stirring constantly, until the mixture thickens. (Do not boil.) Chill until cool and slightly thicker, stirring occasionally.

Fold in the whipped cream. Turn into the prepared mold and chill until set.

Unmold, using Method 3. Garnish with sugar-frosted grapes.

SHERRY-ALMOND SNOW
(4-cup mold, dipped in cold water)

 1 envelope unflavored gelatin
 1 cup cold water
 ½ cup sugar, divided
 Pinch of salt
 3 egg whites
 ¼ cup cream sherry
 ½ teaspoon almond extract

In a small saucepan, sprinkle the gelatin over the cold water and let stand 5 minutes to soften. Add ¼ cup sugar and salt. Place over moderate heat, stirring gently but constantly, until the gelatin is dissolved. Chill until slightly thickened, stirring occasionally.

Beat the egg whites until frothy. Add the remaining sugar and continue beating until stiff but not dry.

Beat the slightly thickened gelatin mixture on high speed until frothy. Beat in the sherry and almond extract. Add the beaten gelatin mixture to the beaten egg whites. Continue beating until well blended. Turn into the prepared mold and chill until set.

Unmold, using Method 1 or 2.

Serve with Custard Sauce (below).

SHERRIED CUSTARD SAUCE
(Yield: 2 cups)

 3 egg yolks
 ¼ cup sugar
 ¼ teaspoon salt
 1¾ cups half-and-half, warmed
 ¼ cup cream sherry

In the top of a double boiler, lightly beat the egg yolks with the sugar and salt. Gradually add the half-and-half and, stirring constantly, cook over hot water until mixture coats a spoon. Do not boil. Remove from heat. Stir in the cream sherry. Cover with plastic wrap while hot to prevent a skin from forming. Chill, covered. Serve cold.

SHERRIED FRUIT CREAM
(6-cup mold, lightly oiled)

      2 envelopes unflavored gelatin
      1 cup cold water
      1/4 cup sugar
      1 can (12 ounces) apricot nectar, chilled
      3/4 cup medium-dry sherry
      2 large peaches
      2 large pears
      1 large banana
      1/4 cup shredded coconut
      1 cup heavy cream, whipped
      Shredded coconut (for garnish; optional)

In a small saucepan, sprinkle the gelatin over the cold water and let stand 5 minutes to soften. Add the sugar and place over medium heat, stirring constantly, until gelatin and sugar are dissolved. Cool slightly.

In a large mixing bowl, combine the dissolved gelatin with the nectar and the sherry. Chill until slightly thickened, stirring occasionally.

Beat the gelatin mixture until frothy. Peel the peaches and pears and cut into bite-size cubes. Immediately stir them into the gelatin mixture. Peel and slice the banana into the mixture. Stir in the 1/4 cup coconut. Fold in the whipped cream. Turn into the prepared mold and chill until set.

Unmold, using Method 3. Garnish with additional coconut, if desired.

SOUR CREAM RING
(6-cup ring mold, lightly oiled)

>1 envelope plus 1½ teaspoons unflavored gelatin
>⅓ cup cold water
>1 cup sugar
>1 cup milk, scalded
>2 cups sour cream
>2 tablespoons kirsch
>1 cup heavy cream, whipped

Soften the gelatin in the cold water for a few minutes. Add the sugar to the hot milk and stir until sugar is dissolved. Add the gelatin and stir until gelatin is dissolved. Set aside to cool.

Add the sour cream and kirsch to the cooled milk. Fold in the whipped cream. Turn into the prepared mold and chill until set.

Unmold, using Method 3.

To serve, fill ring with your favorite berries or other fruit.

FRESH STRAWBERRY MOUSSE
(8-cup mold, lightly oiled)

>1 pint fresh strawberries, washed and halved
>1 pint fresh strawberries, washed and crushed
>¾ cup extra-fine granulated sugar
>¼ cup strawberry liqueur
>2 envelopes unflavored gelatin
>½ cup cold water
>2 cups heavy cream, whipped

Save 8 or 10 strawberries for garnish. Combine the halved berries with the crushed berries, sugar, and liqueur. Let stand at room temperature for about 30 minutes until the sugar is dissolved.

Sprinkle the gelatin over the water in a heat-resistant cup and let stand for 5 minutes to soften. Place cup in a pan of hot water over low heat, stirring until gelatin is dissolved. Add the gelatin to the berries and chill until slightly thickened, stirring occasionally.

Fold in the whipped cream. Turn into the prepared mold and chill until set.

Unmold, using Method 3.

STRAWBERRY ROMANOFF SOUFFLÉ

(4-cup soufflé dish, prepared as instructed on page 12)

  1 pint fresh strawberries, washed and halved
  1 pint fresh strawberries, washed and crushed
  1 cup confectioners' sugar
  2 tablespoons orange-flavored liqueur
  2 envelopes unflavored gelatin
  1 cup cold milk
  2 eggs, separated
  1 teaspoon almond extract
  Red food coloring
  1 cup heavy cream, whipped

Save a few strawberries for garnish. Combine the halved berries with the crushed berries, sugar, and liqueur. Let stand at room temperature.

Sprinkle the gelatin over the milk and let stand for 5 minutes to soften. Lightly beat the egg yolks with the almond extract. Add the softened gelatin. Place over low heat and cook, stirring constantly, until the mixture begins to thicken.

(Do not boil.) Remove from heat. Add a few drops of food coloring. Add the berry mixture to the custard. Chill until slightly thickened, stirring occasionally.

Beat the egg whites until stiff. Fold the whipped cream into the chilled mixture. Fold in the egg whites. Turn into the prepared soufflé dish and chill until set.

To serve, remove the paper collar and garnish with the reserved strawberries.

STRAWBERRY-RHUBARB CHARLOTTE
(9-inch springform pan, 3 inches deep)

> 6 cups rhubarb, cut in ½-inch pieces
> ½ cup sugar
> 1 cup water
> 2 packages (3 ounces each) strawberry-flavored gelatin
> 2 cups heavy cream, whipped
> 1 teaspoon vanilla extract
> 3 dozen ladyfingers, split
> Rhubarb Glaze
> Whole fresh strawberries
> Fresh mint sprigs (optional)

Combine rhubarb and sugar and 1 cup water in a saucepan. Bring to a boil and simmer for 6 to 8 minutes, or until rhubarb is very soft. Drain off 1 cup of syrup and reserve for glaze. Put rhubarb and remaining syrup in a blender to make a pulp (about 3½ cups). Bring pulp to a boil and pour it over the gelatin, stirring until the gelatin is dissolved. Chill until slightly thickened, stirring occasionally. Fold in whipped cream and vanilla.

Line the springform pan with ladyfingers, sides and bottom. Arrange rhubarb mixture with ladyfingers in alternate layers, ending with rhubarb mixture. Chill until set. Remove the springform.

To assemble: Spread the top with ¾ of the Rhubarb Glaze. Split whole strawberries from tip almost to stem end in 4–6 places and open out to resemble petals. Arrange on glaze. Spoon remaining glaze over strawberries. Garnish with mint.

RHUBARB GLAZE

In a saucepan, mix the reserved rhubarb syrup with ¼ cup of sugar. Blend 1½ tablespoons of cornstarch with a small amount of water. Bring the rhubarb syrup to a boil, add the cornstarch, and cook, stirring until thick and clear. Add a few drops of red food coloring, if desired. Cover with plastic wrap and cool.

TANGERINE BAVARIAN
(5-cup mold, lightly oiled)

    1 envelope unflavored gelatin
    1½ cups fresh tangerine juice, divided
    2 eggs, separated
    ½ cup sugar
    Grated rind of 1 tangerine
    1 cup heavy cream, whipped
    Garnish (see below)

Soften the gelatin in ¼ cup of tangerine juice for 5 minutes. In the top of a double boiler, lightly beat the egg yolks with the sugar. Place over hot water, over low heat, and gradually add the remaining tangerine juice, stirring constantly until mixture begins to thicken. Add the softened gelatin, stirring until gelatin is dissolved. Add the tangerine rind. Chill until slightly thickened and cool, stirring occasionally.

Beat the egg whites until stiff. Fold the whipped cream into the chilled mixture. Fold in the egg whites. Turn into the prepared mold and chill until set.

Unmold, using Method 3. Garnish as below.

For garnish, heat until liquid ½ cup red currant jelly and 1 teaspoon tangerine juice. Cool slightly. Dip tangerine sections in mixture and use to decorate unmolded Bavarian.

TAPIOCA RING
(5-cup ring mold, lightly oiled)

1 envelope unflavored gelatin
2 cups milk, divided
2 eggs, separated
⅓ cup sugar
2 tablespoons minute tapioca
¼ teaspoon salt
1 teaspoon vanilla extract
2 teaspoons grated orange rind
2 teaspoons grated lemon rind
¾ cup heavy cream, whipped

Soften the gelatin in ¼ cup of milk for 5 minutes. In a small saucepan, lightly beat the egg yolks with the sugar, tapioca, salt, and vanilla. Place over low heat while gradually adding the remaining 1¾ cups milk. Stir constantly until the mixture comes to a boil. Remove from heat. Add the softened gelatin, stirring until gelatin is dissolved. Add the orange and lemon rinds. Chill until slightly thickened, stirring occasionally.

Beat the egg whites until stiff but not dry. Fold the whipped cream into the chilled tapioca mixture. Fold in the beaten egg whites. Turn into the prepared mold and chill until set.

Unmold, using Method 3.

To serve, fill ring with fresh fruit salad.

VANILLA BAVARIAN CREAM
(4-cup mold, lightly oiled)

2 eggs, separated
4 tablespoons sugar
⅛ teaspoon salt
1½ cups cold milk
1 envelope unflavored gelatin
½ teaspoon vanilla extract
1 cup heavy cream, whipped

Beat the egg yolks, sugar, salt, and cold milk in a medium-sized saucepan. Sprinkle the gelatin on top and let stand 5 minutes to soften. Place over low heat and stir constantly until mixture thickens slightly. Do not boil. Remove from heat and add vanilla. Chill, stirring occasionally, until mixture mounds slightly when dropped from a spoon.

Beat egg whites until stiff. Fold the whipped cream into gelatin mixture. Fold in the egg whites. Turn into the prepared mold and chill until set.

Unmold, using Method 3.

Variations

COFFEE BAVARIAN CREAM

Add 1 tablespoon instant coffee to the saucepan before adding the milk.

Chocolate Bavarian Cream

Add 5 ounces semisweet chocolate morsels to the hot custard before chilling. Stir until melted and well mixed.

Marbled Bavarian Cream

Lightly oil an 8-cup mold. Prepare one batch of either vanilla, coffee, or chocolate Bavarian. Pour into the prepared 8-cup mold and chill.

Immediately prepare a second batch of another flavor. Hold off folding in the whipped cream and egg whites until the first batch (already in the mold) is quite thick but not set. Fold the whipped cream and egg whites into the second batch at this time. Pour the second batch into the mold on top of the first. Gently stir the two together to create a marbled effect. Chill until set.

Unmold, using Method 3.

Chocolate Mint Bavarian

Prepare as for Chocolate Bavarian Cream but substitute ½ teaspoon of peppermint extract for the vanilla.

INTOXICATING DESSERTS

This chapter is a delicious takeoff on some very popular bar drinks. The term "Intoxicating Desserts" is somewhat deceptive as it refers to the senses and not necessarily the alcoholic content of the gelatins. Many of the recipes call for only a small amount of a specific liqueur, just enough for flavoring. Keeping economy in mind, it is possible to purchase most of these alcoholic ingredients in sample-size bottles from your local liquor or package store.

The recipes in this chapter were quite a challenge. Many people are aware of the fact that alcohol does not freeze. The question remained as to whether or not (in a large quantity) it would set in the refrigerator with gelatin added. The puzzle was solved during my experiments when I created a solid block of pure rum gelatin. I was very pleased, for these recipes are not only scrumptious but are also terrific conversation pieces.

APRICOT SOUR SHIMMER
(5-cup mold, dipped in cold water)

2 packages (3 ounces each) lemon-flavored gelatin
1 cup boiling water
2⅓ cups cold water
⅓ cup orange juice
⅓ cup apricot brandy, chilled
1 orange, peeled and sectioned
10 maraschino cherries, halved

Dissolve the gelatin in the boiling water. Add the cold water and orange juice. Chill until very cold and *just beginning**
to thicken. Stir in the apricot brandy.

Pour a thin layer into the bottom of the mold and chill until nearly set.

Using the orange sections and cherry halves, arrange a design on top of the set gelatin. Carefully pour another thin layer of gelatin over the pattern to set the design. Chill until set but not too firm.

Using a rotary beater, beat the remaining gelatin until very fluffy. Turn into the mold, on top of the set pattern. Chill until completely set.

* Alcohol separates; therefore, the gelatin must be of a consistency heavy enough to prevent this yet still loose enough to pour into the mold for the setting of the pattern.

Unmold, using Method 1 or 2. Garnish with orange sections and cherries.

BANANA DAIQUIRI MOUSSE
(7-cup mold, lightly oiled)

2 packages (3 ounces each) lime-flavored gelatin
1 cup boiling water
1½ cups cold water
2 tablespoons grated lime rind
Juice of 1 lime
⅓ cup sugar
½ cup light rum
¼ cup crème de banana
1 ripe banana
1½ cups heavy cream, whipped

Dissolve the gelatin in the boiling water. Add the cold water, rind, juice, and sugar. Mix well. Add the rum and crème de banana. Chill until slightly thickened, stirring occasionally.

Mash the banana and whisk into the thickened gelatin until well blended. Fold in the whipped cream. Turn into the prepared mold and chill until set.

Unmold, using Method 3.

Variation

STRAWBERRY DAIQUIRI MOUSSE

Decrease the cold water to 1 cup. Substitute 1 cup freshly crushed strawberries for the banana. Substitute ¼ cup of strawberry liqueur for the crème de banana.

BANSHEE BAVARIAN
(6-cup mold, lightly oiled

   3 eggs, separated
   ½ cup sugar
   1 cup milk, scalded
   2 envelopes unflavored gelatin
   ¼ cup cold water
   ½ cup crème de banana
   ½ cup white crème de cacao
   1 cup heavy cream, whipped
   Additional whipped cream (for garnish)
   Semisweet chocolate morsels (for garnish)

In a small saucepan, beat the egg yolks with the sugar. Gradually add the scalded milk. Cook over low heat, stirring constantly, until mixture begins to thicken. (Do not boil.) Remove from heat.

Soften the gelatin in the cold water for 5 minutes. Add to the hot custard, stirring until gelatin is dissolved. Transfer to a large mixing bowl. Cool.

Add the crème de banana and crème de cacao. Chill until slightly thickened, stirring occasionally.

Beat the egg whites until stiff. Fold the whipped cream into the thickened custard. Fold in the egg whites. Turn into the prepared mold and chill until set.

Unmold, using Method 3. Garnish with whipped cream and semisweet chocolate morsels.

BLOODY MARY JELL (BREAKFAST DESSERT)
(4-cup mold, dipped in cold water)

2 envelopes unflavored gelatin
3¼ cups tomato juice, divided
2 teaspoons Worcestershire sauce
1 tablespoon lemon juice
¼ teaspoon salt
⅛ teaspoon pepper
1 teaspoon prepared horseradish
½ cup vodka

In a small heat-resistant cup, sprinkle the gelatin over ½ cup of the tomato juice and let stand for 5 minutes to soften. Place cup in a pan of hot water over low heat, stirring until gelatin is dissolved.

Combine the remaining 3 cups of tomato juice with the Worcestershire, lemon juice, salt, pepper, and horseradish. Add the dissolved gelatin, mixing well. Chill until very cold and just beginning to thicken.

Add the vodka, mixing well. Turn into the prepared mold and chill until set.

Unmold, using Method 1 or 2.

Variation

MOCK BLOODY MARY JELL
Omit the vodka and use 3¾ cups tomato juice.

BRANDY ALEXANDER BAVARIAN
(8-cup mold, lightly oiled)

8 egg yolks
1 cup sugar
1½ cups milk, scalded
2 envelopes unflavored gelatin
½ cup cold milk
⅔ cup brandy
½ cup crème de cacao
2 egg whites
1½ cups heavy cream, whipped
Nutmeg

In a small saucepan, beat the egg yolks with the sugar. Gradually add the hot milk. Cook over low heat, stirring constantly, until mixture begins to thicken. (Do not boil.) Remove from heat.

Soften the gelatin in the cold milk for 5 minutes. Add to the hot custard and stir until gelatin is dissolved. Cool slightly, stirring occasionally to prevent a skin from forming on the surface. Transfer to a large mixing bowl.

Add the brandy and crème de cacao to the cooled mixture. Chill until slightly thickened, stirring from time to time.

Beat the egg whites until stiff. Fold the whipped cream into the cold custard. Fold in the egg whites. Turn into the prepared mold and chill until set.

Unmold, using Method 3. Sprinkle with nutmeg.

EGGNOG RING
(5-cup ring mold, lightly oiled)

4 eggs, separated
1 envelope unflavored gelatin
½ cup sugar
⅛ teaspoon salt
1 cup cold milk
½ cup rum
1 cup heavy cream, whipped
Nutmeg

In a saucepan, lightly beat the egg yolks with the gelatin, sugar, and salt. Add the cold milk, mixing well. Place over low heat, stirring constantly, until the mixture thickens slightly. (Do not boil.) Remove from heat and cool slightly.

Stir in the rum. Chill until slightly thickened, stirring occasionally.

Beat the egg whites until stiff but not dry. Fold the whipped cream into the custard mixture. Fold in the beaten egg whites. Turn into the prepared mold and chill until set.

Unmold, using Method 3. Sprinkle with nutmeg.

GOLDEN CADILLAC MOUSSE
(7-cup mold, lightly oiled)

6 egg yolks
⅔ cup sugar
1½ cups milk, scalded
2 envelopes unflavored gelatin
¼ cup cold water
¼ cup Galliano liqueur
½ cup white crème de cacao
2 cups heavy cream, whipped

In the top of a double boiler, beat the egg yolks with the sugar. Gradually add the scalded milk, stirring constantly. Cook over hot (not boiling) water until thickened.

Soften the gelatin in the cold water. Add to the hot custard and stir until gelatin is dissolved. Set aside to cool slightly.

Add the Galliano and the crème de cacao. Fold in the whipped cream. Turn into the prepared mold and chill until set.

Unmold, using Method 3.

GOLDEN DREAM SOUFFLÉ
(4-cup soufflé dish, prepared as instructed on pages 12–13.)

3 eggs, separated
1 cup sugar
Pinch of salt
2 envelopes unflavored gelatin
1½ cups orange juice
3 tablespoons grated orange rind
⅓ cup Galliano liqueur
¼ cup orange-flavored liqueur
2 cups heavy cream, whipped

In a small saucepan, beat the egg yolks with the sugar, salt, and gelatin. Add the orange juice and cook over low heat, stirring constantly, until mixture thickens. (Do not boil.) Remove from heat and cool slightly.

Add the orange rind and both liqueurs. Chill until slightly thickened, stirring occasionally.

Beat the egg whites until stiff but not dry. Fold the whipped cream into the chilled custard. Fold in the beaten egg whites. Turn into the prepared soufflé dish and chill until set.

Do not unmold. Simply remove paper collar before serving.

GRASSHOPPER SOUFFLÉ
(4- to 5-cup soufflé dish, prepared as instructed on pages 12–13.)

8 egg yolks
1 cup sugar
2 cups milk, scalded
2 envelopes unflavored gelatin
½ cup cold water
⅓ cup green crème de menthe
⅓ cup white crème de cacao
Green food coloring
2 cups heavy cream, whipped
Additional whipped cream (for garnish)
Semisweet chocolate (for garnish)

In the top of a double boiler, beat the egg yolks with the sugar. Gradually add the scalded milk. Cook over hot (not boiling) water, stirring constantly until thickened. Soften the gelatin in the cold water for 5 minutes. Add to the hot custard, stirring until gelatin is dissolved. Set aside to cool, stirring occasionally to prevent a skin from forming on the surface.

Add the crème de menthe and crème de cacao to the cooled custard. Add a few drops of food coloring for a rich color. Fold in the whipped cream. Turn into the prepared dish and chill until set.

Do not unmold this dish. To serve, remove the paper collar. Garnish with whipped cream and shaved chocolate curls or chocolate morsels.

HARVEY WALLBANGER SHIMMER
(5-cup mold, dipped in cold water)

2 envelopes unflavored gelatin
3½ cups orange juice
¼ cup vodka, chilled
¼ cup Galliano liqueur, chilled
2 oranges, peeled and sectioned
1 orange, sliced (for garnish)

Sprinkle the gelatin over ½ cup of orange juice in a small heat-resistant cup and let stand for 5 minutes to soften. Place cup in a pan of hot water over low heat, stirring until gelatin is dissolved.

Add the dissolved gelatin to the remaining 3 cups orange juice. Chill until very cold and *just beginning** to thicken. Stir in the vodka and the Galliano. Pour a thin layer into the bottom of the mold and chill until set but not too firm.

Using the orange sections, arrange a design on top of the set gelatin. Carefully ladle another layer of gelatin over the design to set the pattern. Chill until set but not too firm.

Beat the remaining gelatin with a rotary beater until very fluffy. Turn into the mold, on top of the set pattern. Chill until completely set.

Unmold, using Method 1 or 2. Garnish with orange sections.

---

* Alcohol separates; therefore, the gelatin must be of a consistency heavy enough to prevent this yet still loose enough to pour into the mold for the setting of the pattern.

IRISH COFFEE LAYERED MOUSSE
(6-cup mold, lightly oiled)

 2 envelopes plus 1 teaspoon unflavored gelatin
 3⅔ cups cold black coffee
 ½ cup sugar
 ⅓ cup Irish whiskey
 1 tablespoon grated orange rind
 1 cup heavy cream, whipped

In a small saucepan, sprinkle the gelatin over ⅔ cup of coffee and let stand for 5 minutes to soften. Add the sugar and place over low heat, stirring until gelatin and sugar are dissolved. Add to the remaining 3 cups of cold coffee. Stir in the whiskey and the orange rind. Chill until slightly thickened, stirring occasionally.

Put 2 cups of the slightly thickened mixture into a mixing bowl. Fold in the whipped cream. Turn into the prepared mold and chill until nearly set. In the meantime, keep the remaining thickened mixture at room temperature.

When the mold has nearly set, carefully add to the top of it the remaining thickened mixture of coffee. When unmolded, this will be at the bottom, with the creamy mixture on top. Chill the mold until set.

Unmold, using Method 3.

JACK ROSE SHIMMER
(5-cup mold, dipped in cold water)

 2 packages (3 ounces each) lime-flavored gelatin
 1 cup boiling water
 2½ cups cold water
 1 tablespoon grenadine
 ⅓ cup applejack, chilled
 1 Delicious (red) apple, cored

Dissolve the gelatin in the boiling water. Add the cold water and grenadine. Chill until very cold and *just beginning** to thicken. Stir in the applejack. Pour a thin layer into the bottom of the mold and chill until set but not too firm.

Thinly slice the apple and arrange a design on top of the set gelatin. Carefully ladle another layer of gelatin over the pattern to set the design. Make sure the apples are completely covered with gelatin, so that they do not turn brown. Chill until set but not too firm.

Using a rotary beater, beat the remaining gelatin until very fluffy. Turn into the mold, on top of the set pattern. Chill until completely set.

Unmold, using Method 1 or 2.

MAI TAI MOUSSE
(8-cup mold, lightly oiled)

6 eggs, separated
1½ cups sugar
½ cup lime juice
⅓ cup lemon juice
½ cup maraschino cherry liquid
Pinch of salt
¼ cup orange liqueur
¼ cup light rum
¼ cup dark rum
2 envelopes unflavored gelatin
2 cups heavy cream, whipped
Pineapple slices (for garnish)
Maraschino cherries (for garnish)

---

* Alcohol separates; therefore, the gelatin must be of a consistency heavy enough to prevent this yet still loose enough to pour into the mold for the setting of the pattern.

Beat the egg yolks with the sugar. Add the juices, cherry liquid, and salt. Cook over low heat, stirring constantly until thickened. Do not boil.

Combine the liqueur and light and dark rums. Sprinkle the gelatin on top to soften. Stir into the hot yolk mixture until gelatin is dissolved. Set aside to cool.

Beat the egg whites until stiff. Fold the whipped cream into the cooled custard. Fold in the egg whites. Turn into the prepared mold and chill until set.

Unmold, using Method 3. Garnish with pineapple slices and maraschino cherries.

PERNOD MOUSSE
(7-cup mold, lightly oiled)

6 egg yolks
1 cup sugar
1½ cups milk, scalded
2 envelopes gelatin
¼ cup cold water
¼ cup Pernod
¼ cup white crème de cacao
2 cups heavy cream, whipped
Shaved chocolate (for garnish)

In the top of a double boiler, beat the egg yolks with the sugar. Gradually add the scalded milk. Cook over hot water, stirring constantly until thickened. Soften the gelatin in the cold water. Add to the hot custard and stir until gelatin is dissolved. Set aside to cool.

Add the Pernod and the white crème de cacao. Fold in the whipped cream. Turn into the prepared mold and chill until set.

Unmold, using Method 3. Garnish with shaved chocolate.

PIÑA COLADA MOUSSE
(4-cup mold, lightly oiled)

    1 envelope plus 1 teaspoon unflavored gelatin
    ¼ cup cold water
    1 cup canned pineapple juice*
    ½ cup cream of coconut
    ¼ cup rum
    1 cup heavy cream, whipped
    Pineapple slices (for garnish)
    Maraschino cherries (for garnish)

Sprinkle the gelatin over the water in a small heat-resistant cup and let stand for 5 minutes to soften. Place cup in a pan of hot water over low heat, stirring until gelatin is dissolved.

Combine the pineapple juice, cream of coconut, and rum. Add the gelatin. Chill until slightly thickened, stirring occasionally.

Beat the thickened gelatin until smooth. Fold in the whipped cream. Turn into the prepared mold and chill until set.

Unmold, using Method 3. Garnish with pineapple slices and cherries.

PINK LADY SOUFFLÉ
(4-cup soufflé dish, prepared as instructed on pages 12–13.)

    2 packages (3 ounces each) lemon-flavored gelatin
    1 cup boiling water
    3 eggs, separated
    ⅛ teaspoon salt
    ½ cup apple juice

* Do not use fresh or frozen pineapple juice as it does not jell correctly.

½ cup gin
¼ cup apple brandy
2 tablespoons grenadine
Red food coloring
1½ cups heavy cream, whipped
Additional whipped cream (for garnish; optional)

Dissolve the gelatin in the boiling water. In a small saucepan, beat the egg yolks, salt, and apple juice. Gradually add the hot gelatin, stirring constantly. Cook over low heat until the mixture thickens slightly, but do not boil. Remove from heat. Cool. Transfer to a large mixing bowl.

Stir in the gin, apple brandy, grenadine, and a few drops of red food coloring. Chill until slightly thickened, stirring occasionally.

Beat the egg whites until stiff. Fold the whipped cream into the thickened gelatin. Fold in the egg whites. Turn into the prepared soufflé dish and chill until set.

Do not unmold. To serve, simply remove paper collar. Garnish with whipped cream, if desired.

PINK SQUIRREL MOUSSE
(7-cup mold, lightly oiled)

6 egg yolks
½ cup sugar
1 cup milk, scalded
2 envelopes unflavored gelatin
¼ cup cold water
½ cup crème de almond or crème de noyau
½ cup white crème de cacao
Red food coloring
2 cups heavy cream, whipped
Slivered, blanched almonds (for garnish)
Chocolate morsels (for garnish)

In the top of a double boiler, lightly beat the egg yolks with the sugar. Gradually add the scalded milk. Cook over hot water, stirring constantly, until the mixture begins to thicken. (Do not boil mixture.)

Soften the gelatin in the cold water for 5 minutes. Add to the hot mixture, stirring until gelatin is dissolved. Cool.

Add the crème de almond and crème de cacao. Add a few drops of red food coloring until the mixture is bright pink. Chill until cold and slightly thickened, stirring occasionally.

Fold in the whipped cream. Turn into the prepared mold and chill until set.

Unmold, using Method 3. Garnish with almonds and chocolate morsels.

SANGRIA FRUIT SHIMMER
(8-cup mold, dipped in cold water)

3 envelopes unflavored gelatin
¾ cup orange juice
¼ cup lemon juice
½ cup sugar
3 cups red wine, divided
2 tablespoons orange-flavored liqueur
2 tablespoons brandy
1 cup club soda
2 oranges, peeled and sectioned
3 medium peaches, peeled and sliced
1 cup fresh strawberries, halved

In a medium-sized saucepan, sprinkle the gelatin over the combined orange and lemon juices and let stand for 5 minutes to soften. Add the sugar and 1 cup red wine. Place over low heat, stirring until gelatin is dissolved. Cool.

Add the remaining wine, liqueur, brandy, and soda. Pour a thin layer into the bottom of the mold and chill until set but not too firm. Using a few choice pieces of fruit, arrange a design on top of the set gelatin. Ladle another layer of gelatin over the fruit, to cover, and chill to set the pattern.

Chill the remaining gelatin until slightly thickened, stirring occasionally.

Halve the remaining orange sections and peach slices. Fold into the thickened gelatin. Fold in the strawberries. Turn into the mold and chill until set.

Unmold, using Method 1 or 2.

WHITE RUSSIAN BAVARIAN
(6-cup mold, lightly oiled)

3 eggs, separated
½ cup sugar
1 cup milk, scalded
2 envelopes unflavored gelatin
¼ cup cold water
½ cup white crème de cacao
⅔ cup vodka
1 cup heavy cream, whipped
Shaved chocolate (for garnish)

In the top of a a double boiler, beat the egg yolks with the sugar. Gradually add the scalded milk. Cook over hot (not boiling) water, stirring constantly until thickened.

Soften the gelatin in the cold water. Add to the hot custard and stir until gelatin is dissolved. Set aside to cool.

Add the crème de cacao and the vodka. Chill until slightly thickened.

Beat the egg whites until stiff. Fold the whipped cream gently into the cooled custard. Fold in the egg whites. Turn into the prepared mold and chill until set.

Unmold, using Method 3. Garnish with shaved chocolate.

CALORIE CONTROL AND DIET CONSCIOUSNESS

Gelatin is often associated with dieting. However, a close look at the ingredients contained in many of the recipes in this book certainly alters that idea. Some of the recipes, especially the ones that contain cream, are, indeed, high in calories. However, remember that they are also very rich and are therefore served only in small portions. If you prepare these dishes only occasionally or for special parties, the calories can be overlooked. These recipes are really no higher in calorie content than many other standard dishes commonly served.

For the unfortunate few, however, who absolutely must stick to strict diets for various reasons, there are substitutions that can be made. They will slightly alter the flavor of the recipe, but in most cases, you will still be left with a delicious and attractive dish. So don't despair. As long as you do not change the quantities, you may go ahead with whatever changes are necessary. Following are some substitutions that you may want to use:

sugar—may be omitted
heavy cream— dessert topping or evaporated skim milk
    (1 cup heavy cream = 2 cups whipped)
salt—omit or use substitute
flavored gelatin—diet flavored gelatin
mayonnaise—imitation mayonnaise
sour cream—imitation sour cream
cream cheese—imitation cream cheese
butter—margarine

All of the above, although closely similar to the "real thing," still have a noticeably different flavor to those who are not accustomed to using them. Therefore, unless you have just cause for making such alterations, the best flavor is still to be obtained by using the original ingredient.

In addition to providing guidelines for substitutions, this chapter contains a few bonus low-calorie recipes. You will notice that although many of these recipes are of the creamy type, the preparation of the mold only requires dipping in cold water, rather than the usual method of lightly oiling. This is, of course, necessary in order to omit as many calories as possible. These gelatins may still be unmolded by using Method 3. If, however, you would feel more secure when unmolding by using the oiled mold, the calorie content will still remain low with the use of safflower oil.

APPLE SLIMMER SAUCE MOLD
(3-cup mold, dipped in cold water)

1 envelope plus 1 teaspoon unflavored gelatin
¼ cup natural orange juice

2 tablespoons lemon juice
2 cups dietetic applesauce, divided
1/4 teaspoon cinnamon
2 egg whites

Sprinkle the gelatin over the combined orange and lemon juices and let stand for 5 minutes to soften. In a small saucepan, combine 1 cup of applesauce and cinnamon. Bring to a boil, stirring, then remove from heat. Add the softened gelatin and stir until gelatin is dissolved. Add the remaining 1 cup applesauce. Chill until cool and slightly thickened, stirring occasionally.

Beat the egg whites until stiff. Fold into the thickened mixture. Turn into the prepared mold and chill until set.

Unmold, using Method 1 or 2.

DOUBLE CHEESE DIET RING

(3-cup ring mold, dipped in cold water)

1 envelope unflavored gelatin
1/2 cup cold skim milk
1/2 cup skim milk, heated to boiling
3 ounces imitation cream cheese, room temperature
1 1/2 cups low-fat cottage cheese
1/2 teaspoon almond extract
2 teaspoons grated lemon rind

In a blender, sprinkle gelatin over cold milk and let stand for 5 minutes to soften. Add hot milk and process at low speed for 2 minutes. Dice cream cheese and blend a little at a time until smooth. Add cottage cheese and remaining ingredients;

process at high speed for 2 minutes. Turn into the prepared mold and chill until set.

Unmold, using Method 1 or 2.

To serve, fill ring with fresh blueberries and strawberries.

Variation

DOUBLE CHEESE PINEAPPLE MOLD

Omit almond extract and lemon rind. Fold in 1 can (8 ounces) crushed pineapple (unsweetened), drained, to the mixture after the final blending. Increase size of mold to 4-cup capacity.

VERY CHERRY RICE MOUSSE
(5-cup cold, dipped in cold water)

1 package (3 ounces) cherry-flavored diet gelatin
1 cup boiling water
1 can (8 ounces) dietetic dark cherries
1½ cups cold cooked rice
⅔ cup evaporated skim milk
1 tablespoon lemon juice

Dissolve the gelatin in the boiling water. Drain the juice from the cherries into the gelatin. Chill until slightly thickened.

Cut the cherries into quarters. Mix with the rice. Pour the milk (undiluted) into a medium-sized metal bowl and place in the freezer until ice crystals form (partially frozen). Chill beaters in the refrigerator. Add the lemon juice and beat until thick. If the milk does not whip, it is not cold enough and needs further chilling. Continue beating until stiff. Mix the rice and cherries into the thickened gelatin. Fold in the whipped milk. Turn into the prepared mold and chill until set.

Unmold, using Method 3.

Note: Other fruit flavors may be substituted for the gelatin and cherries.

LOW-CAL CHICKEN SALAD ASPIC
(4 individual molds, dipped in cold water)

4 large slices of tomato ($\frac{1}{2}$ inch thick)
Vinegar
Salt and pepper
1 envelope unflavored gelatin
$\frac{1}{4}$ cup cold water
2 chicken bouillon cubes
$1\frac{2}{3}$ cups boiling water
3 tablespoons imitation mayonnaise
2 tablespoons minced green pepper
2 tablespoons minced celery
1 teaspoon minced chives
12 blanched almonds, slivered
$1\frac{1}{2}$ cups chopped cooked chicken breast

Marinate the tomatoes in vinegar seasoned with salt and pepper. Cover and refrigerate.

Soften gelatin in the cold water for 5 minutes. Add bouillon cubes to the boiling water and stir until cubes are dissolved. Add the softened gelatin and stir until gelatin is dissolved. Pour a thin layer of gelatin mixture into the bottom of each mold and chill. Chill the remaining gelatin until slightly thickened.

Add the remaining ingredients to the thickened gelatin mixture. Turn into the prepared aspic molds. Chill until set.

Unmold, using Method 4, and place each mold on a slice of tomato.

MOLDED CRAB SALAD
(4-cup mold, dipped in cold water)

1 envelope unflavored gelatin
⅔ cup cold water
2 tablespoons white wine vinegar
¼ cup imitation mayonnaise
1 cup plain low-fat yogurt
12 ounces fresh or frozen cooked crab meat, drained and
    cleaned
2 carrots, peeled and shredded
¼ cup minced parsley
1 teaspoon cayenne pepper
2 teaspoons grated lemon rind
3 large cloves garlic, crushed

In a small heat-resistant cup, sprinkle the gelatin over the water and let stand for 5 minutes to soften. Place cup in a pan of hot water over low heat, stirring until gelatin is dissolved. Add to the vinegar, mayonnaise, and yogurt, mixing well.

In a mixing bowl, combine the remaining ingredients, tossing until thoroughly mixed. Fold into the yogurt mixture. Turn into the prepared mold and chill until set.

Unmold, using Method 3.

Serve with salad greens.

HONEY-AND-APPLE YOGURT MOUSSE
(5-cup mold, dipped in cold water)

1 envelope plus 1½ teaspoons unflavored gelatin
¼ cup unsweetened apple juice
2 eggs, separated
1 cup skim milk
¼ cup honey
16 ounces plain low-fat yogurt
1 large red apple

Soften the gelatin in the apple juice. In a small saucepan, lightly beat the egg yolks. Add the skim milk, mixing well. Place over low heat, stirring constantly, until the mixture begins to thicken. Do not let it boil or the mixture will curdle. Add the softened gelatin to the hot mixture. Add the honey and stir well until gelatin and honey are dissolved. Chill until slightly thickened.

Remove thickened mixture from refrigerator and beat until smooth. Add the yogurt and continue beating until well mixed. Using the largest hole of a grater, grate the apple (including skin) directly into the mixture. Stir. Beat the egg whites until stiff. Fold into the mixture. Turn into the prepared mold and chill until set.

Unmold, using Method 3.

LOW-CAL FRUIT BAVARIAN
(4-cup mold, dipped in cold water)

1 package (3 ounces) fruit-flavored diet gelatin
½ cup boiling water
1 can (8 ounces) dietetic fruit (to correspond with flavor of
    gelatin)
¼ teaspoon almond extract
½ cup skim milk powder
½ cup cold water
2 teaspoons lemon juice

Dissolve the gelatin in the boiling water. Purée the fruit with juice in a blender. Add dissolved gelatin and almond extract. Process for 10 seconds or until well mixed. Turn into a bowl and chill until slightly thickened, stirring occasionally.

Combine milk powder with cold water and lemon juice. Chill.

Beat until stiff. Beat the thickened gelatin mixture until smooth. Fold in the whipped milk. Turn into the prepared mold and chill until set.

Unmold, using Method 3.

Note: This recipe may be converted into a Charlotte Russe by lining a straight-sided 5- or 6-cup mold with ladyfingers. In this case, it is not necessary to dip the mold in cold water. Simply pour the whipped gelatin mixture into the center of the mold. Unmold, using Method 1 or 2.

MANDARIN MOUSSE
(5-cup mold, dipped in cold water)

1 envelope plus 1½ teaspoons unflavored gelatin
¼ cup natural orange juice

2 eggs, separated
1 cup skim milk
¼ cup honey
16 ounces plain low-fat yogurt
1 teaspoon vanilla extract
½ teaspoon ground cardamom
2 cans (8 ounces each) mandarin orange sections, dietetic
Toasted sliced blanched almonds

Soften the gelatin in the orange juice. In a small saucepan, lightly beat the egg yolks with the skim milk. Place over low heat, stirring constantly, until the mixture begins to thicken slightly. (Do not let it boil.) Remove from heat. Add the softened gelatin and the honey to the hot mixture and stir well until gelatin and honey are dissolved. Chill until slightly thickened.

Remove thickened mixture from refrigerator and beat until smooth. Add the yogurt, vanilla extract, and cardamom and continue beating until well mixed. Drain the orange sections and slice each in half. Fold into the mixture. Beat the egg whites until stiff. Fold in. Turn into the prepared mold and chill until set.

Unmold, using Method 3. Sprinkle with sliced almonds.

PINEAPPLE-MINT MOLD
(5-cup mold, dipped in cold water)

1 can (20 ounces) unsweetened crushed pineapple
½ cup cold water
2 envelopes unflavored gelatin
2 cups buttermilk
¼ teaspoon mint extract
⅛ teaspoon green food coloring
Mint leaves (for garnish)

Drain the liquid from the pineapple and combine it with the cold water in a small saucepan. Sprinkle the gelatin over the top and let stand for 5 minutes to soften. Place over low heat, stirring until gelatin is dissolved. Cool.

Add the buttermilk, mint extract, and coloring. Taste for sweetness. Chill until slightly thickened, stirring occasionally.

Fold in the crushed pineapple. Turn into the prepared mold and chill until set.

Unmold, using Method 1 or 2. Garnish with mint leaves.

LOW-CAL THOUSAND ISLAND CHEF SALAD MOLD
(5-cup mold, dipped in cold water)

1 envelope unflavored gelatin
12 ounces dietetic tomato juice
½ cup imitation mayonnaise
¼ cup vinegar
1 tablespoon sweet pickle relish
1 clove garlic, crushed
1½ cups finely chopped cold cooked chicken breast
½ cup finely chopped Swiss cheese
1 hard-cooked egg, peeled and chopped
2 tomatoes, peeled, seeded, and chopped
½ cup finely chopped green bell pepper
1 onion, sliced thin (for garnish)

In a small saucepan, sprinkle the gelatin over the tomato juice and let stand for 5 minutes to soften. Place over low heat and stir until gelatin is dissolved. Cool slightly.

Add the mayonnaise and vinegar and chill until slightly thickened, stirring occasionally.

Mix in the relish and garlic. Fold in the chicken, cheese,

egg, tomatoes, and pepper. Turn into the prepared mold and chill until set.

Unmold, using Method 1 or 2. Garnish with thin slices of onion.

Serve with salad greens.

LOW-CAL TUNA SALAD MOLD
(2½-cup fish mold, dipped in cold water)

1 envelope unflavored gelatin
¼ cup cold water
1¼ cups boiling water
2 chicken bouillon cubes
1 teaspoon lemon juice
⅓ cup imitation mayonnaise
1 tablespoon chopped onion
1 tablespoon chopped parsley
1 stalk celery, diced
1 can (7 ounces) tuna, packed in water, drained

Soften the gelatin in the cold water for 5 minutes. Add the boiling water and bouillon cubes and stir until gelatin and cubes are dissolved.

Place remaining ingredients in a blender and process at low speed for 5 seconds. Add half the gelatin-bouillon mixture to the blender and process until mixed. Add the remaining bouillon mixture and process at high speed for 10 seconds, or until well blended and chopped. Turn into the prepared mold and chill until set.

Unmold, using Method 3.

NATURAL FOODS AND
VEGETARIAN DIETS

There are many people who eat only naturally grown foods. Many of the recipes in this book can be converted simply by substituting natural products. This chapter contains a few additional recipes that natural-food lovers may enjoy.

Gelatin is made from collagen, which is animal protein obtained from bones, skin, and connective tissues. Gelatin has no flavor and also contains no sugar, and therefore is often used in the preparation of natural foods.

Agar-agar is a natural seaweed with jelling properties. It is flaky in appearance. Vegetarians who eat no animal products whatsoever may use agar-agar for preparing molded dishes. Some people claim that, measure for measure, its thickening powers are greater or more concentrated than gelatin's. I, however, have not found this to be so and therefore recommend that agar-agar be measured in exactly the same amounts as you would ordinary gelatin. In other words, 1 tablespoon agar-agar for every 2 cups of liquid called for in a recipe. Agar-agar is more difficult to dissolve than gelatin. The liquid in a recipe must be brought to a full boil. The agar-agar is then sprinkled over the boiling liquid and must cook for 5 minutes in order to completely dissolve. Because it is more costly, more time-consuming to prepare, and because many vitamins are lost in the boiling process, I would suggest that agar-agar be used only in preparing pure vegetarian meals. It may, in this case, be substituted for the gelatin in any of the appropriate recipes in this book.

CURRIED BROWN-RICE-AND-CARROT MOLD
(5-cup mold, lightly oiled)

1 teaspoon each: ground cloves, cumin, ginger, sea salt, and turmeric
¼ teaspoon cayenne pepper
1 envelope unflavored gelatin
¼ cup cold water
1½ cups yogurt
2 cups cooked brown rice
1 cup shredded carrots
½ cup seedless raisins
1 teaspoon finely minced onion

Make a curry powder by combining the 6 spices mentioned above. In a small heat-resistant cup, sprinkle the gelatin over the water and let stand for 5 minutes to soften. Place cup in a pan of hot water over low heat, gently stirring until gelatin is dissolved. Stir the dissolved gelatin into the yogurt, mixing well. Beginning with 1 teaspoon, add the curry mixture to the yogurt to taste. Combine the rice, carrots, raisins, and onion. Fold into the curried yogurt. Turn into the prepared mold and chill until set.

Unmold, using Method 3.

TOMATO–ROSE HIP ASPIC
(6-cup mold, dipped in cold water)

3 envelopes unflavored gelatin
2½ cups tomato juice, divided
½ cup rose hips
3 cups water
1 tablespoon lemon juice
Lettuce (for garnish)

Soften the gelatin in 1 cup of the tomato juice for 5 minutes. Combine the rose hips and water in a saucepan. Bring to a boil and simmer gently for 15 minutes. Strain, discarding the rose hips, and return the liquid to the saucepan. Add the softened gelatin. Place over low heat, stirring until the gelatin is dissolved. Add the lemon juice and remaining tomato juice. Mix well. Turn into the prepared mold and chill until set.

Unmold, using Method 1 or 2. Garnish with lettuce.

Note: Up to 1 cup of chopped vegetables may be added to the aspic. Before turning into the prepared mold, chill the mixture until slightly thickened, stirring occasionally. Stir in the chopped vegetables. Turn into the mold and chill until set.

CAROB MOUSSE
(5- to 6-cup mold, lightly oiled)

2 envelopes unflavored gelatin
2½ cups cold milk, divided
2 tablespoons honey
½ cup carob powder
1 teaspoon pure vanilla extract
1½ cups heavy sweet cream, whipped
Shredded unsweetened coconut (for garnish)
Wheat germ (for garnish)

In a small heat-resistant cup, sprinkle the gelatin over ½ cup cold milk and let stand for 5 minutes to soften. Place cup in a pan of hot water over low heat, gently stirring until gelatin is dissolved. Combine the dissolved gelatin with the remaining cold milk, honey, carob powder, and vanilla extract. Beat until well blended. Chill until slightly thickened, stirring occasionally.

Beat the slightly thickened gelatin until frothy. Fold in the whipped cream. Turn into the prepared mold and chill until set.

Unmold, using Method 3. Sprinkle with the coconut and wheat germ.

Serve with additional whipped cream, if desired.

YOGURT FRUIT WHIP
(4- to 6-cup mold, lightly oiled)

1 envelope unflavored gelatin
¼ cup cold fruit juice
1½ cups puréed fresh fruit
1 tablespoon honey
1 teaspoon pure vanilla or almond extract
Pinch sea salt
1½ cups plain yogurt

In a small heat-resistant cup, sprinkle the gelatin over the juice and let stand for 5 minutes to soften. Place cup in a pan of hot water over low heat, gently stirring until gelatin is dissolved. Combine the dissolved gelatin with the purée, honey, vanilla extract, and salt. Mix well. Chill until slightly thickened, stirring occasionally.

Beat with a rotary or electric beater, about 5 minutes at high speed, or until light and fluffy. Fold in the yogurt. Turn into the prepared mold and chill until set.

Unmold, using Method 3.

DO YOUR OWN THING

Once you have made a few of the recipes in this book and are familiar with the sturdiness and various textures of gelatins, and you have acquired confidence in unmolding, you may wish to create some of your own recipes. As you may now realize, there are unlimited combinations of food that can be jelled.

This chapter gives you some basic recipes to which you may add your own choice of ingredients. And below is a basic gelatin formula with which you might like to experiment from scratch.

You should find it helpful to reread pages 14 through 17 to refresh your memory on some of the basic points of gelatin cookery.

BASIC GELATIN FORMULA

1 envelope of unflavored gelatin or 1 package (3 ounces) flavored gelatin will jell the following:

> 2 cups liquid
> plus: 1 cup of mayonnaise, whipped or sour cream
> plus: 1½–2 cups solid ingredients, chopped or ground

Note: If you wish to double or triple this basic formula, the liquid and semisolid (creamy) ingredients must be decreased to compensate for the additional volume as follows:

2 envelopes gelatin
3½ cups liquid
1½ cups semisolid (creamy) ingredients
3–4 cups solid ingredients

or

3 envelopes gelatin
5 cups liquid
2 cups semisolid (creamy) ingredients
5–5½ cups solid ingredients

Some additional useful information:

1 envelope of unflavored gelatin = 3 teaspoons
1 cup of heavy cream, whipped = 2 cups (heavy cream doubles in size when whipped)
1 egg white, depending on various factors, when beaten will increase about 5 to 8 times in volume

Always season quite heavily before adding cream, mayonnaise, or egg whites to your gelatin, in order to compensate for their blandness.

Canned pineapple, mangoes, and papayas are preferred for use in gelatin recipes. If you wish to use the fresh or frozen product, boil it for 3 minutes before adding it in the recipe. The same pertains to juice from these fruits. They all contain an enzyme that resists the jelling process unless they are first cooked.

Finally, at the end of this chapter, there is a Table of Measurements that will be useful in creating your own recipes.

SALAD ASPIC—BASIC RECIPE
(3½-cup mold, dipped in cold water)

    1 envelope unflavored gelatin
    ¼ cup cold water
    2 tablespoons sugar
    ½ teaspoon salt
    2 tablespoons vinegar or wine
    2 tablespoons lemon juice
    1½ cups fruit juice or consommé
    1½ cups chopped vegetables or fruit

Sprinkle the gelatin over the water in a small heat-resistant bowl and let stand for 5 minutes to soften. Add the sugar, salt, vinegar, and lemon juice. Place bowl in a pan of hot water over low heat, stirring until gelatin, sugar, and salt are dissolved. Add to the 1½ cups fruit juice or consommé, stirring well. Chill until slightly thickened, stirring occasionally.

Add the 1½ cups of chopped vegetables or fruit. Turn into the prepared mold and chill until set.

Unmold, using Method 1 or 2.

VEGETABLE ASPIC—BASIC RECIPE
(4-cup mold, dipped in cold water)

2 envelopes unflavored gelatin
½ cup cold water
3¼ cups V-8 or tomato juice
2 tablespoons lemon juice
1 tablespoon Worcestershire sauce
Salt and pepper to taste
1 cup sour cream (optional) or 1 cup mayonnaise (optional) or ½ cup mayonnaise and ½ cup heavy cream, whipped (optional)*
1–2 cups chopped vegetables, eggs, meats, fish, or a combination of these

In a small heat-resistant cup, sprinkle the gelatin over the water and let stand for 5 minutes to soften. Place cup in a pan of hot water over low heat, stirring until gelatin is dissolved. Add dissolved gelatin to the tomato juice, lemon juice, Worcestershire, salt and pepper and taste for seasoning. Chill until slightly thickened. This amount will fill a 4-cup mold. (If you do not plan to add any other ingredients, chill the gelatin until set.)

When slightly thickened, add your choice of ingredients as listed above and increase the size of the mold according to the quantity you are adding.

Turn into the prepared mold and chill until set.

Unmold, using Method 1 or 2, or Method 3 if using cream or mayonnaise.

---

* It is not necessary to add the optional cream or mayonnaise, but if you do, remember to increase the size of your mold to hold the additional amount. Also remember to lightly grease your mold.

CREAMY SALAD MOLD—BASIC RECIPE
(4-cup mold, lightly oiled)

1 envelope unflavored gelatin
1 cup cold chicken broth, divided
1 tablespoon prepared mustard
1 tablespoon grated onion
1 teaspoon Worcestershire sauce
2 hard-cooked egg yolks, forced through sieve
½ cup mayonnaise
½ cup sour cream
1½–2 cups additional ingredients: chopped vegetables, eggs, meats, seafood, or a combination of these
Salt and pepper to taste

Sprinkle gelatin over ¼ cup of chicken broth in a small heat-resistant cup and let stand for 5 minutes to soften. Place cup in a pan of hot water over low heat, stirring until gelatin is dissolved. Add to remaining ¾ cup of chicken broth. Add the mustard, onion, Worcestershire, and egg yolks; mix well. Add the mayonnaise and sour cream. Chill until slightly thickened, stirring occasionally.

Add the additional ingredients with salt and pepper to taste. Turn into the prepared mold and chill until set.

Unmold, using Method 3.

SAVORY MOUSSE—BASIC RECIPE
(6-cup mold, lightly oiled)

1 envelope unflavored gelatin
¼ cup cold water
1 tablespoon butter
1 tablespoon flour
1 cup milk
¼ cup wine, red or white
1 tablespoon chopped parsley
1 tablespoon grated onion
1½ cups chopped cooked meat or seafood
½ cup chopped vegetables
½ cup mayonnaise
Salt and pepper to taste
1 cup heavy cream, whipped

Sprinkle the gelatin over the water in a small dish and let stand for 5 minutes to soften. Melt the butter in a small saucepan. Add the flour and stir well. Gradually add the milk, stirring constantly over low heat, until the mixture begins to thicken. Add the softened gelatin to the hot sauce and stir until gelatin is dissolved. Remove from heat and cool slightly.

Add the wine. Chill until slightly thickened, stirring occasionally.

Add the parsley, onion, and chopped ingredients. Add the mayonnaise and mix well. Add salt and pepper to taste. Fold in the whipped cream. Turn into the prepared mold and chill until set.

Unmold, using Method 3.

FRUIT JUICE WHIP—BASIC RECIPE
(6-cup mold, dipped in cold water)

 1 envelope unflavored gelatin
 2 cups fruit juice, divided*
 3 tablespoons sugar
 1 teaspoon grated rind (optional)
 2 egg whites, *un*beaten

Sprinkle the gelatin over 1/4 cup of fruit juice in a small heat-resistant cup and let stand for 5 minutes to soften. Add the sugar and place cup in a pan of hot water over low heat, stirring until gelatin and sugar are dissolved. Add the remaining 1¾ cups fruit juice. Add rind, if desired. Chill until slightly thickened.

Remove from refrigerator and beat until frothy. Add the unbeaten egg whites and continue beating until fluffy and tripled in volume. Turn into the prepared mold and chill until set.

Unmold, using Method 1 or 2.

Serve with Custard Sauce (page 161), Sherried Custard Sauce (page 192), or light cream.

---

* Do not use lemon juice alone, as it is too strong. When combining lemon juice with other juices or water, it will be necessary to increase the amount of sugar to taste.

DESSERT MOUSSE—BASIC RECIPE
(6-cup mold, lightly oiled)

 1 envelope unflavored gelatin
 ¼ cup cold water or juice
 3 egg yolks
 ½ cup sugar
 1 cup milk, scalded
 1 teaspoon flavored extract or ¼ cup flavored liqueur
 1 teaspoon grated rind (optional)
 1½ cups chopped or puréed fruit*
 1 cup heavy cream, whipped

Soften the gelatin in the cold water. In the top of a double boiler, beat the egg yolks with the sugar. Gradually add the milk, constantly stirring. Place over hot (not boiling) water, stirring until the mixture begins to thicken. Add the softened gelatin, stirring until gelatin is dissolved. Remove from heat. Add the extract or liqueur and the rind, if used. Chill until slightly thickened, stirring occasionally.

Add the fruit. Fold in the whipped cream. Turn into the prepared mold and chill until set.

Unmold, using Method 3.

SWEET BAVARIAN—BASIC RECIPE
(8-cup mold, lightly oiled)

 Basic Recipe for Dessert Mousse (above)
 2 egg whites

Make the Basic Recipe for Dessert Mousse; however, after folding in the whipped cream, beat the egg whites until stiff

* If the fruit is puréed, increase the amount of gelatin by 1½ teaspoons.

and fold into the mousse as the final ingredient. Turn into the prepared mold and chill until set.

Unmold, using Method 3.

DESSERT SOUFFLÉ—BASIC RECIPE
(4- to 5-cup soufflé dish)

Make the Basic Recipe for Sweet Bavarian (above). Tie a paper collar around the soufflé dish so that it extends 4 inches above the dish (see pages 12–13). It is not necessary to oil or treat the dish in cold water, since this type of dessert is not unmolded. To serve, simply remove the paper collar.

TABLE OF MEASUREMENTS

3 teaspoons	1 tablespoon
2 tablespoons	1 fluid ounce
4 tablespoons	¼ cup or 2 fluid ounces
5⅓ tablespoons	⅓ cup
16 tablespoons	1 cup or 8 fluid ounces
2 cups	1 pint
2 pints	1 quart
4 quarts	1 gallon
1 pound	16 ounces
1 cup heavy cream	2 cups whipped cream
1 stick butter	½ cup
4 ounces cheese (hard)	1 cup shredded
1 small lime (Key)	1½–2 tablespoons juice
1 lime (Persian)	3 tablespoons juice
1 lemon	2–3 tablespoons juice
1 orange	6–7 tablespoons juice or ⅓–½ cup juice

METRIC CONVERSIONS

Lists of ingredients for each recipe in this book have been given in American standard measures. However, in certain cases, metric measures may be desired.

If you should decide to convert any of these recipes to metric, it is important to convert every ingredient listed. Never mix American standard and metric in the same recipe. For example, the measurement of 1 cup appears to be the same in both American standard and metric. Although the word "cup" is the same, the quantity is slightly different. The American standard yield is approximately 10 percent less than the equivalent metric yield. Therefore, after converting a recipe to metric measure, be sure to use metric measuring utensils.

Following is a useful chart for making the necessary conversions.

Spoonfuls

¼ teaspoon	1.25 milliliters
½ teaspoon	2.5 milliliters
¾ teaspoon	3.75 milliliters
1 teaspoon	5 milliliters
2 teaspoons	10 milliliters
1 tablespoon	15 milliliters

Cups

¼ cup	59 milliliters
⅓ cup	78 milliliters
½ cup	118 milliliters
⅔ cup	157 milliliters
¾ cup	177 milliliters
1 cup	236 milliliters

Fluid Ounces

¼ ounce	7.5 milliliters
½ ounce	15 milliliters
1 ounce	30 milliliters

Pints, Quarts, Gallons

½ pint	236 milliliters
1 pint	473 milliliters
1 quart	946.3 milliliters
1 gallon	3,785 milliliters

Weight in Ounces

¼ ounce	7.1 grams
½ ounce	14.17 grams
¾ ounce	21.27 grams
1 ounce	28.35 grams

Pounds

¼ pound	.113 kilogram
½ pound	.227 kilogram
¾ pound	.340 kilogram
1 pound	.454 kilogram
2.2 pounds	1 kilogram

INDEX

accompaniments, *see* Relishes and accompaniments

alcoholic beverages, recipes using, *see* brandy (brandied); desserts using wines, liqueurs, etc.; ported; sherry (sherried); wines, recipes using

almond
Bavarian, with macaroons, 156
macaroons, 156–57

anchovy-artichoke aspic, 22

appetizers, 21
anchovy-artichoke aspic, 22
caviar mousse, 22–23
caviar-salmon mousse, 43–44
celery remoulades, molded, 23–24
chicken diablo mousse, 25
chicken liver pâté, brandied, 26–27
clam dip mousse, 27
clam mousse, cottage, 28–29
clam ring, 28
crabmeat quiche, 41
cream cheese–horseradish mousse, 36
egg cups, curried, 31
egg mousse, 30–31
egg salad mold, and variation, 33–34
eggs with asparagus mousse, 32
eggs in avocado mousse, individual, 32–33
guacamousse, 34–35
ham, parslied (jambon persillé), 37
herb mousse, fresh, 35–36
horseradish–cream cheese mousse, 36
jambon persillé, 37
liverwurst mousse in aspic, 38
onion mousse, creamy, 39
pâté mousse, 39–40
quiche Lafayette, molded, and variations, 40–41
red and white ring, 42
Roquefort cheese mousse, 43
salmon–caviar mousse, 43–44
salmon mousse with shrimp, 44–45
shrimp in brandied aspic, 46
shrimp quiche, 41
shrimp-and-tomato cream mousse, 46–47
smoked salmon mousse, 45
Spanish quiche, 41
three cheese ring, 24
wine consommé molds, individual, 47

apple
-and-blackberry mousse, 162
-chestnut mousse, 148–49
-chicken mousse, curried, 51–52
mousse, fresh, 157–58
salad, molded, 110–11
slimmer sauce mold, 220–21

applesauce
mousse, fresh, 158–59
-orange ring, 153
slimmer sauce mold, 220–21

apricot
jelly roll mousse, 159–61
nectar Bavarian, 182
sour shimmer, 202–3
surprise, molded, 111–12

artichoke
-anchovy aspic, 22
hearts in wine aspic, 89–90
asparagus mousse (I, II), 90–91
mousse, eggs with, 32
aspics, basic recipes
salad, 237
vegetable, 238
aspics, for decorating salads and
savories
basic, 136–37
beef, Madeira, 138
caviar, speckled, 139
citrus, speckled, 137
fish, no-stock, 137–38
leftover, 127, 128
Madeira beef, 138
herb, speckled, 138–39
quick, 135
quick wine, 135
speckled caviar, 139
speckled citrus, 139
speckled herb, 138–39
turned-out gelatins, method for,
127–29
wine, quick, 135
within-mold method, 125–27
avocado
-grapefruit mold, 117
guacamousse, 34–35
mousse (I, II), 92–93
mousse, crab meat in, layered
with tomato aspic, 72–73
mousse, eggs, individual, in, 32–
33
-pineapple salad, 112–13

banana
Daiquiri mousse, and variation,
203
-nut mousse, 113–14
banshee Bavarian, 204

basic recipes, 235
Bavarian, sweet, 243
gelatin formula, 236–37
mousse, dessert, 242
mousse, savory, 240
salad aspic, 237
salad mold, creamy, 239
vegetable aspic, 238
whip, fruit juice, 241
Bavarian (Bavarian cream)
almond, with macaroons, 156
banshee, 204
brandy Alexander, 206
chestnut, brandied, 167–68
coconut, 170–71
coffee ricotta, 171–72
double cheese, 166–67
fruit, low-cal, 226
Nesselrode ricotta, 178–79
orange-cherry, 179–80
pear nectar, and variations, 181–
182
pumpkin—Thanksgiving Day
delight, 186–87
raspberry, easy, and variations,
187–88
sweet, basic recipe, 242–43
tangerine, 197–98
vanilla, and variations, 199–200
white Russian, 217–18
beef
à la mode, jellied, 49–50
aspic, Madeira, 138
beet borscht salad mold, 94–95
Bing cherry salad, 114
blackberry-and-apple mousse, 162
Bloody Mary jell, 205
mock, 205
blueberry mousse, ported, 162–63
brandy (brandied)
Alexander Bavarian, 206
aspic, shrimp in, 46
beef à la mode, jellied, 49–50

chestnut Bavarian, 167–68
chicken liver pâté, 26–27
meat loaf aspic, 63
pâté mousse, 39–40
broccoli mousse, 95–96
brown-rice-and-carrot mold, curried, 231–32

cabbage: coleslaw, molded, 99–100
calorie-control and diet-consciousness recipes, 219–20
  apple slimmer sauce mold, 220–221
  chef salad, low-cal Thousand Island mold, 228–29
  chicken salad aspic, low-cal, 223–224
  crab salad, molded, 224
  double cheese diet ring, 221–22
  fruit Bavarian, low-cal, 226
  honey-and-apple yogurt mousse, 225
  mandarin mousse, 227
  pineapple-mint mold, 227–28
  tuna salad mold, low-cal, 229
  very cherry rice mousse, 222–23
caper
  mousse, 148
  sauce, dilled, 84–85
caramel mousse, 163–64
carob mousse, 233
carrot
  -and-brown-rice mold, curried, 231–32
  mousse, 96
  mousse, minted, 97
  shredded, gelatin, 98
cauliflower-tomato aspic, 98–99
caviar
  aspic, speckled, 139
  mousse, 22–23

-salmon mousse, 43–44
celery remoulades, molded, 23–24
charlotte
  butter cream, 165
  defined, 12
  marbled plum, 184–85
  mold for, 12
  pineapple, 182–83
  russe au Grand Marnier, 166
  strawberry-rhubarb, 196–97
chaud-froid, decorating with, 127–129
  leftover chaud-froid, 129
  lime sauce, jellied, and variations, 140
  mayonnaise, jellied, and variations, 141–42
  white sauce, jellied, 142–43
cheese
  Bavarian, coffee ricotta, 171–72
  Bavarian, double-cheese, 166–67
  Bavarian, nesselrode ricotta, 178–79
  cottage cheese–pineapple mold, 123–24
  cottage clam mousse, 28–29
  cottage potato ring, 104
  cream cheese–horseradish mousse, 36
  double, diet ring, 221–22
  -and-ham mousse, 60–61
  red and white ring, 42
  Roquefort cheese mousse, 43
  Roquefort chef salad mousse, 65–66
  three-cheese ring, 24
chef salad
  Roquefort mousse, 65–66
  Thousand Island mold, low-cal, 228–29
cherry
  -orange Bavarian cream, 179–80
  rice mousse, very cherry, 222–23

chestnut
-apple mousse, 148–49
Bavarian, brandied, 167–68
chicken
-almond salad, citrus ring with,
50–51
-apple mousse, curried, 51–52
diablo mousse, 25
lemon chicken-and-zucchini
mousse, 53
liver pâté, brandied, 26–27
mousse, 52
salad aspic, low-cal, 223–24
tarragon mousse, 54
-and-zucchini mousse, lemon, 53
chocolate
Bavarian cream, 200
mint Bavarian, 200
pinwheel, double, 168–70
citrus
aspic, speckled, 139
ring with chicken-almond salad,
50–51
salad ring, fresh, 114–15
clam
dip mousse, 27
mousse, 71
mousse, cottage, 28–29
ring, 29
coconut Bavarian cream, 170–71
coffee
Bavarian cream, 199
Bavarian ricotta, 171–72
Irish, layered mousse, 211
coleslaw, molded, 99–100
corned beef salad, molded, 55
cottage cheese
clam mousse, 28–29
-pineapple mold, 123–24
potato ring, 104
red and white ring, 42

crab meat
in avocado mousse layered with
tomato aspic, 72–73
quiche, 41
salad, molded, 73, 224
cranapple fruit relish, jellied,
150–151
cranberry
cream, jellied, 150
fruit salad, 116
whip, molded, 186
cream cheese–horseradish mousse,
36
creamy onion mousse, 39
cucumber(s)
mousse, minted, 101
in yogurt mold, 100
curried
apple-chicken mousse, 51–52
brown-rice-and-carrot mold, 231–
232
egg cups, 31
custard sauce, 161, 192–93

Daiquiri mousse
banana, 203
strawberry, 203
decorating
turned-out gelatin, 127–34
within mold, 16, 125–27
decorating desserts, 144–45
frosting cream, stabilized, 145–
146
decorating salads and savories, 125
aspic, leftover, 127, 129
aspic, within-mold method, 125–
127
aspic recipes for, 135–39
chaud-froid, leftover, 129
chaud-froid method, 127–29
chaud-froid recipes for, 140–43

decorations, 129–31
decorations, medallions as, 131–134
decorations, pastry-bag, 134
turned-out gelatins, 127–34
within mold, 125–27
desserts, 155
almond Bavarian with macaroons, 156
apple-and-blackberry mousse, 162
apple mousse, fresh, 157–58
applesauce mousse, fresh, 158–159
apple slimmer sauce mold, 220–221
apricot jelly roll mousse, 159–161
Bavarian (*see also* Bavarian; names; ingredients), basic sweet, 242–43
blackberry-and-apple mousse, 162
caramel mousse, 163–64
carob mousse, 233
charlotte butter cream, 165
charlotte russe au Grand Marnier, 166
charlotte, *see also* charlotte; names
coconut Bavarian cream, 170–71
decorating, 144–46
double cheese Bavarian, 166–67
fruit Bavarian, low-cal, 226
"intoxicating" (*see also* desserts using wines, liqueurs, etc.), 201–18
lemon-and-lime mousse, layered, 174–75
lemon or lime snow pudding, fresh, 173–74
marbled plum charlotte, 184–85

mousse, basic recipe (*see also* ingredients, names), 242
orange-cherry Bavarian cream, 179–80
papaya mousse, 180–81
pear nectar Bavarian, and variations, 181–82
pineapple charlotte, 182–83
pineapple-mint mold, 227–28
prune whip, molded, and variations, 185–86
pumpkin Bavarian—Thanksgiving Day delight, 186–87
raspberry Bavarian, easy, and variations, 187–88
rhubarb mousse, fresh, 188–89
rice mousse, very cherry, 222–23
soufflé, basic recipe (*see also* soufflé; names), 242
strawberry-rhubarb charlotte, 196–97
tangerine Bavarian, 197–98
tapioca ring, 198–99
vanilla Bavarian cream, and variations, 199–200
whip, basic recipe, 241
yogurt fruit whip, 234
desserts using wines, liqueurs, etc.
apricot sour shimmer, 202–3
banana Daiquiri mousse, and variation, 203
banshee Bavarian, 204
Bloody Mary jell, and variation, 205
blueberry mousse, ported, 162–163
brandy Alexander Bavarian, 206
chestnut Bavarian, brandied, 167–68
coffee ricotta Bavarian, 171–72
double chocolate pinwheel, 168–170

desserts using wines, liqueurs, etc.
(*Continued*)
eggnog ring, 207
fig mousse, 172
ginger mousse, 173
golden Cadillac mousse, 207–8
golden dream soufflé, 208–9
grasshopper soufflé, 209
Harvey Wallbanger shimmer, 210
"intoxicating," 201–18
Irish coffee layered mousse, 211
Jack Rose shimmer, 211–12
macedoine mousse of fresh fruits, 176
Mai Tai mousse, 212–13
Maltaise rice mousse, 177
maple mousse, 178
Nesselrode ricotta Bavarian, 178–79
Pernod mousse, 213
piña colada mousse, 214
pink lady soufflé, 214–15
pink squirrel mousse, 215–16
pistachio mousse Christmas wreath, 183–84
rice mousse, Maltaise, 177
riz à l'impératrice, 190–91
rosé sabayon mousse, 191
sangría fruit shimmer, 216–17
sherried fruit cream, 193–94
sherry-almond snow, 192
sour cream ring, 194
strawberry mousse, fresh, 194–95
strawberry Romanoff soufflé, 195–96
White Russian Bavarian, 217–218
diet consciousness, *see* calorie-control and diet-consciousness recipes
dilled caper sauce, 84–85
dill mayonnaise, chaud-froid, 142

doing your own thing, 235–43
double cheese
Bavarian, 166–67
diet ring, and variation, 221–22
double chocolate pinwheel, 168–170
Doyle's salmon mousse, 84
duck
layered, with apricots, 56–57
layered, with cherries in aspic, 56
layered, with oranges, 57
mousse with peaches in aspic, 57–58

egg(s)
in avocado mousse, individual, 32–33
with asparagus mousse, 32
cups, curried, 31
curried, cups, 31
curried salad mold, 34
-and-eel aspic, 74
mousse, 30–31
quiche, *see* quiche
salad mold, 33–34
salad mold, curried, 34
eggnog ring, 207
eel-and-egg aspic, 74

fig mousse, 172
fish
aspic, no-stock, 137–38
mousse, 75
see also Main courses—seafood; names of fish, shellfish
frosting cream, stabilized, 145–46
fruit(s)
Bavarian, low-cal, 226
cream, sherried, 193–94
juice whip, basic, 241
macedoine mousse of fresh, 176
nectar salad, 116–17

salads, *see* Fruit salads
sangría shimmer, 216–17
yogurt whip, 234
see also names of fruits
fruit salads, 110
apple, molded, 110–11
apricot surprise, molded, 111–12
avocado-grapefruit mold, 117
avocado-pineapple, 112–13
banana-nut mousse, 113–14
Bing cherry, 114
citrus salad ring, fresh, 114–15
cranberry, 116
decorating (*see also* decorating
salads and savories), 125–43
fruit nectar salad, 116–17
grapefruit-avocado mold, 117
grapefruit mist, 118
green-grape, frosty, 119–20
green grape-lime mousse with
fresh fruits, 118–19
melon-ball, 120–21
orange-pineapple gelatin, 121–
122
pear mousse, spiced, 122
pineapple-avocado salad, 112–13
pineapple–cottage cheese mold,
123–24
pineapple cream, molded, 123
pineapple-orange gelatin, 121–
122
Waldorf mousse, 124

gazpacho salad mold, 101–2
gelatin formula, basic, 236–37
ginger mousse, 173
golden Cadillac mousse, 207–8
golden dream soufflé, 208–9
goose mousse with apples in aspic,
ported, 58–59
grapefruit
-avocado mold, 117
mist, 118

grapes, *see* green grape
grasshopper soufflé, 209
green bean mousse, fresh, 102–3
green grape
-lime mousse with fresh fruits,
118–19
salad, frosty, 119–20
guacamousse, 34–35

haddock mousse, 76
ham
with apples in aspic, 59–60
-and-cheese mousse, 60–61
-and-cider mousse, 61–62
mousse, 62
parslied (jambon persillé), 37
Harvey Wallbanger shimmer, 210
herb mousse, fresh, 35–36
herbed green mayonnaise, chaud-
froid, 142
herring salad ring, 77
honey-and-apple yogurt mousse,
225
horseradish
-cream cheese mousse, 36
cream, molded, 151

"intoxicating" desserts (*see also*
desserts using wines, liqueurs,
etc.), 201–3
Irish coffee layered mousse, 211

Jack Rose shimmer, 211–12
jambon persillé, 37
jellied
beef à la mode, 49–50
chaud-froid, 140–43
cranapple fruit relish, 150–51
cranberry cream, 150
pigs knuckles, 64–65
tongue ring, 66
jellied chaud-froid
lime sauce, 140

jellied chaud-froid (*Continued*)
  mayonnaise, and variations,
    141–42
  white sauce, 142–43
jelly roll
  apricot mousse, 159–61
  double chocolate pinwheel, 168–
    170

layered
  duck with cherries in aspic, and
    variations, 56–57
  lemon-and-lime mousse, 174–75
layering mixtures, 15–16
lemon
  chicken-and-zucchini mousse, 53
  -and-lime mousse, layered, 174–
    175
  snow pudding, fresh, 173–74
lime
  -and-lemon mousse, layered, 174–
    175
  sauce, chaud-froid jellied, and
    variations, 140
  snow pudding, fresh, 173–74
liqueurs and liquors, *see* alcoholic
    beverages, recipes using; des-
    serts using wines, liqueurs, etc.
liverwurst mousse in aspic, 38
lobster mousse, 78
low-cal
  chef salad mold, Thousand
    Island, 228–29
  chicken salad aspic, 223–24
  fruit Bavarian, 226
  tuna salad, mold, 229
  see also calorie-control and diet-
    consciousness recipes

macaroons, almond, 156–57
Madeira beef aspic, 138

main courses—meats, 48–59
  apple-chicken mousse, curried,
    51–52
  beef à la mode, jellied, 49–50
  brandied meat loaf aspic, 63
  chef salad, low-cal Thousand
    Island mold, 228–29
  chef salad mousse, Roquefort,
    65–66
  chicken-almond salad, citrus ring
    with, 50–51
  chicken-apple mousse, curried,
    51–52
  chicken mousse, 52
  chicken mousse, tarragon, 54
  chicken salad aspic, low-cal, 223–
    224
  chicken-and-zucchini mousse,
    lemon, 53
  citrus ring with chicken-almond
    salad, 50–51
  corned beef salad, molded, 55
  duck with cherries in aspic, lay-
    ered, and variations, 56–57
  duck mousse with peaches in
    aspic, 57–58
  goose mousse with apples in
    aspic, ported, 58–59
  ham with apples in aspic, 59–60
  ham-and-cider mousse, 61–62
  ham-and-cheese mousse, 60–61
  ham mousse, 62
  jellied beef à la mode, 49–50
  jellied pigs knuckles, 64–65
  jellied tongue ring, 66
  layered duck with cherries in
    aspic, and variations, 56–57
  lemon chicken-and zucchini
    mousse, 53
  meat loaf aspic, brandied, 63
  pigs knuckles, jellied, 64–65
  ported goose mousse with apples
    in aspic, 58–59

Roquefort chef salad mousse, 65–66
tarragon chicken mousse, 54
tongue ring, jellied, 66
turkey-cranberry mousse, 67–68
veal and olives in wine aspic, 69
veal salad, molded, 68–69
Vienna potato salad, 70
main courses—seafood, 48–49
clam mousse, 71
crab meat in avocado mousse layered with tomato aspic, 72–73
crab meat salad, molded, 73
crab salad, molded, 224
Doyle's salmon mousse, 84
eel-and-egg aspic, 74
fish mousse, fresh, 75
haddock mousse, 76
herring salad ring, 77
lobster mousse, 78
mussel chowder mousse, 78–80
mussels marinière aspic, 80–81
octopus in aspic, 81–82
oyster mousse, fresh, 83
salmon mousse, Doyle's, 84
scallops in aspic, 82
seafood salad, molded, 85–86
smoked trout mousse, 86–87
trout mousse, 86–87
tuna salad, molded, 87
tuna salad mold, low-cal, 229
Mai Tai mousse, 212–13
Maltaise rice mousse, 177
mandarin mousse, 226–27
maple mousse, 178
marbled
Bavarian cream, 200
plum charlotte, 184–85
mayonnaise, chaud-froid jellied, and variations, 141–42
measurements, table of, 243
metric conversions, 244

meat loaf aspic, brandied, 63
meats, *see* main courses—meats; names of dishes, meats
medallions, decorating with, 131–134
melon-ball salad, 120–21
minted
carrot mousse, 97
cucumber mousse, 101
molds, choosing and preparing, 11–13
mousse, basic recipe
dessert, 242
savory, 240
see also main ingredients
mushrooms in aspic, 103
mussel(s)
chowder mousse, 78–80
marinière aspic, 80–81
mustard
cream cup, 152
mayonnaise, chaud-froid, 141
mousse, 152–53

natural foods and vegetarian diet recipes, 230–31
brown-rice-and-carrot mold, curried, 231–32
carob mousse, 233
tomato–rose hip aspic, 232
nectar whip, molded, 186
Nesselrode ricotta Bavarian, 178–179
no-stock fish aspic, 137–38

octopus in aspic, 81–82
onion mousse, creamy, 39
orange(s)
-applesauce ring, 153
-cherry Bavarian cream, 179–80
mandarin mousse, 226–27
-pineapple gelatin, 121–22
oyster mousse, fresh, 83

Papaya mousse, 180–31
pâté mousse, 39–40
peach
  Bavarian, 188
  nectar Bavarian, 182
pear
  mousse, spiced, 122
  nectar Bavarian, and variations,
    181–82
pecan-squash mold, 107–8
Pernod mousse, 213
pigs knuckles, jellied, 64–65
piña colada mousse, 214
pineapple
  -avocado salad, 112–13
  Bavarian, 188
  charlotte, 182–83
  –cottage cheese mold, 123–24
  cream molded, 123
  double cheese mold, 222
  -mint mold, 227–28
  -orange gelatin, 121–22
pink lady soufflé, 214–15
pink squirrel mousse, 215–16
pistachio mousse Christmas
    wreath, 183–84
plum charlotte, marbled, 184–85
ported
  blueberry mousse, 162–63
  goose mousse with apples in
    aspic, 58–59
potato
  cottage ring, and variation, 104
  salad, molded, 105
  salad, Vienna, 70
prune whip, molded, and varia-
    tions, 185–86
pumpkin Bavarian—Thanksgiving
    Day delight, 186–87

quiche
  Lafayette, molded, 40–41
  Lorraine, 41

crabmeat, 41
shrimp, 41
Spanish, 41

raspberry Bavarian, easy, and
    variations, 187–88
red-and-green rice salad mold, 106
red and white ring, 42
relishes and accompaniments, 147
  applesauce-orange ring, 153
  caper mousse, 148
  chestnut-apple mousse, 148–49
  cranapple fruit, jellied, 150–51
  cranberry cream, jellied, 150
  horseradish cream, molded, 151
  mustard cream cup, 152
  mustard mousse, 152–53
  orange-applesauce ring, 153
  tartar sauce mousse, 154
rhubarb
  mousse, fresh, 188–89
  -strawberry charlotte, 196–97
rice
  brown-rice-and-carrot mold, cur-
    ried, 231–32
  mousse, Maltaise, 177
  mousse, very cherry, 222–23
  riz à l'impératrice, 190–91
  salad mold, red-and-green, 106
ricotta Bavarian
  coffee, 171–72
  Nesselrode, 178–79
riz à l'impératrice, 190–91
Roquefort
  cheese mousse, 43
  chef salad mousse, 65–66
rose hip–tomato aspic, 232
rosé sabayon mousse, 191

salad(s), molded
  aspic, basic recipe, 237

creamy, basic recipe, 239
decorating (*see also* decorating
   salads and savories), 125–43
see also fruit salads; main ingredients
salmon
   -caviar mousse, 43–44
   mousse, Doyle's, 84
   mousse, with shrimp, 44–45
   smoked, mousse, 45
sangría fruit shimmer, 216–17
savory mousse, basic recipe, 240
scallops in aspic, 82
seafood
   mayonnaise, chaud-froid, 142
   salad, molded, 85–86
   see also fish; main courses—sea-
      food; names
sherry (sherried)
   almond snow, 192
   fruit cream, 193–94
shellfish, *see* names
shredded carrot gelatin, 98
shrimp
   in brandied aspic, 46
   quiche, 41
   -and-tomato cream mousse, 46–47
smoked salmon mousse, 45
smoked trout mousse, 86–87
snow (snow pudding)
   lemon or lime, fresh, 173–74
   sherry-almond, 192
soufflé
   defined, 12
   dessert, basic recipe, 243
   golden dream, 208–9
   grasshopper, 209
   mold for, 12–13
   pink lady, 214–15
   strawberry Romanoff, 195–96
sour cream
   potato ring, 104
   ring, 194

speckled aspic
   caviar, 139
   citrus, 139
   herb, 138–39
spiced pear mousse, 122
spinach salad, molded, 106–7
squash-pecan mousse, 107–8
strawberry
   Bavarian, 188
   Daiquiri mousse, 203
   mousse, fresh, 194–95
   -rhubarb charlotte, 196–97
   Romanoff soufflé, 195–96

tangerine Bavarian, 197–98
tapioca ring, 198–99
tarragon chicken mousse, 54
tartar sauce mousse, 154
Thousand Island chef salad mold,
   low-cal, 228–29
three-bean salad mold, 93–94
three-cheese ring, 24
tips and techniques
   chilling to thicken slightly, 15
   chilling until firm, 16–17
   covering, 16–17
   decorating salads and savories
      (*see also* decorating salads and
      savories), 125–43
   decorating turned-out gelatin,
      127–34
   decorating within mold, 16, 125–
      127
   dissolving gelatin, 15
   folding in, 17
   freezing, 17
   grating ingredients, 17
   layering mixtures, 15–16
   measurements, 243–44
   molds, choosing and preparing,
      11–13
   softening gelatin, 14–15

tips and techniques (*Continued*)
unmolding, 18–20
whipping or beating, 17
tomato aspic
crab meat in avocado mousse layered with, 72–73
ring, 108
–rose hip, 232
tongue ring, jellied, 66
trout mousse, smoked, 86–87
tuna salad molded, 87
low-cal, 229
turkey-cranberry mousse, 67–68

unmolding, 18–20

vanilla Bavarian cream, with variations, 199–200
veal
and olives in wine aspic, 69
salad, molded, 68–69
vegetable aspic, basic recipe, 238
vegetable molds, 88
asparagus mousse (I, II), 90–91
artichoke hearts in wine aspic, 89–90
avocado mousse, (I, II), 92–93
beet borscht salad mold, 94–95
broccoli mousse, 95–96
carrot gelatin, shredded, 98
carrot mousse, 96
carrot mousse, minted, 97
cauliflower-tomato aspic, 98–99
coleslaw, molded, 99–100
cucumber mousse, minted, 101
cucumbers in yogurt mold, 100
gazpacho salad mold, 101–2
green bean mousse, fresh, 102–3

mushrooms in aspic, 103
potato ring, cottage, and variation, 104
potato salad, molded, 105
rice salad mold, red-and-green, 106
spinach salad, molded, 106–7
squash-pecan mousse, 107–8
three-bean salad mold, 93–94
watercress Vichyssoise mold, 109
see also names of vegetables
vegetarian diets, *see* natural foods and vegetarian diets
very cherry rice mousse, 222–23
Vienna potato salad, 70

Waldorf salad mousse, 124
watercress Vichyssoise mold, 109
whip
fruit juice, basic recipe, 241
prune, and variations, 185–86
yogurt fruit, 234
White Russian Bavarian, 217–18
white sauce, chaud-froid
jellied, 142–43
wines, recipes using
aspic, artichoke hearts in, 89–90
aspic, quick, 135
consommé molds, individual, 47
desserts using, *see* desserts using wines, liqueurs, etc.
orange-pineapple gelatin, 121–22

yogurt
fruit whip, 234
honey-and-apple mousse, 225
mandarin mousse, 226–27